The Person of Christ

THE PERSON OF CHRIST

by
LORAINE BOETTNER, D.D.

AUTHOR OF

The Reformed Doctrine of Predestination;

The Inspiration of the Scriptures;

The Christian Attitude Toward War;

A Summary of the Gospels;

The Atonement.

WIPF & STOCK · Eugene, Oregon

Wipf and Stock Publishers
199 W 8th Ave, Suite 3
Eugene, OR 97401

The Person of Christ
By Boettner, Loraine
ISBN 13: 978-1-60608-924-8
Publication date 8/5/2009
Previously published by Eerdmans, 1943

The Person of Christ

CONTENTS

I. Introduction 9
II. Christ's Own Testimony Concerning His Deity.. 12
III. Testimony of the Apostles 17
IV. Titles Ascribed to Jesus Christ 24
V. The Son of God 30
VI. The Son of Man 36
VII. The Pre-existence of Christ 39
VIII. The Attributes of Deity Are Ascribed to Christ.. 44
IX. Jesus' Life the Fulfillment of a Divine Plan 61
X. The Miracles of Jesus 69
XI. Importance of Belief in the Deity of Christ 74
XII. The Humanity of Christ 79
XIII. The Humiliation of Christ 90
XIV. The Exaltation of Christ 93
XV. The Relation of the Two Natures in Christ 101
XVI. The Incarnation 113
XVII. The Sinlessness of Jesus 123
XVIII. The Virgin Birth 128
XIX. Christ the Messiah of the Old Testament 137
XX. The Personal Appearance of Jesus 165
XXI. The Offices of Christ 173
XXII. Erroneous Views Concerning the Person
of Christ 201
XXIII. Conclusion 211

I.

INTRODUCTION

PROBABLY the most earnestly discussed question in religious circles today is, "What Is Christianity?" But before we can reach a conclusion concerning that question we must settle another which is vitally related to it, namely, "Who Was, or Who Is Jesus Christ?"

There is practically unanimous agreement that a person bearing this name once walked the earth and that the movement which we know as Christianity sprang from Him. There is also practically unanimous agreement that for the last nineteen hundred years His influence has been the most potent and uplifting of all influences in shaping and moulding the life of our western world.

That Jesus was the finest speciment of humanity that the world has ever known, that His teachings were the purest and loftiest that the world has ever received, and that His actions were the most faultless that the world has ever seen, is admitted by practically every one. But from the time He walked the earth until this present hour there has been no end of controversy concerning His person and concerning the place that He occupies in the religion that He founded. More specifically the controversy has to do with the question whether Jesus was as the Scriptures represent Him to have been, the second person of the Trinity, God incarnate, who is to be worshipped and obeyed even as the Father, or whether He was only a man endowed with unusual spiritual insight, differing from other men not in kind but only in degree, and occupying a place in the Christian system not essentially different from that which Confucius occupies in Confucianism or Mohammed in Mohammedanism.

Historically the first great question that came up in the early Church had to do with the Person of Christ. The Church settled that question for herself once and for all by affirming that He is the divine Son of God, Diety incarnate. That decision was written into her authoritative creeds, and ever since that time Evangelical Christianity has been bold to assert that "The Church's one foundation is Jesus Christ her Lord." And this faith has been expressed not only in the creeds, but in the hymns and in the devotional writings of her representative spokesmen. Protestants and Catholics alike agree that Christ saves, although they differ in their opinions as to how He saves.

In comparatively recent times, however, — we may even say within the lifetime of our own generation — the faith of the Church has been seriously challenged not only from without but from within. The result is that today even among those who call themselves Christians there is no general agreement either as to who Christ is or as to what He does for our salvation. This in turn has led to endless confusion not only between denominations but also within individual churches. The doctrine of the Person of Christ is, therefore, not merely one of a number of equally important doctrines, but the most central and basic of the entire system, the very corner-stone of the temple of truth which is set forth in the Scriptures. We would define Christianity as that redemptive religion which offers salvation from sin, through the expiatory death of Christ, sin being conceived of as guilt and power and pollution. And, consequently, we hold that to admit the Diety of Christ and to trust Him for salvation constitutes one a Christian, and that to reject His Deity marks one a non-Christian. The purpose of this book is to present the evidence which we believe is abundantly sufficient to prove that Christ was indeed Diety incarnate, the eternal Son of God, who came to this earth in order that He might provide a way of redemption for sinful men.

II.

CHRIST'S OWN TESTIMONY CONCERNING HIS DEITY

THE most important witness to the Deity of Christ is, of course, Christ Himself. The New Testament records make it abundantly clear that He possessed not only a sense of unbroken fellowship with God but a distinct consciousness that He Himself was God. From the age of twelve at least, when in reply to His mother's question He said, "How is it that ye sought me? knew ye not that I must be in my Father's house?", this sense appears, and it later becomes one of the dominant notes of His doctrine. He expressly claims equality with God the Father. "I and the Father are one," John 10:30. "He that hath seen me hath seen the Father," John 14:9. " . . . that all may honor the Son, even as they honor the Father. He that honoreth not the Son honoreth not the Father that sent Him," John 5:23. "He that believeth on me, believeth not on me, but on Him that sent me. And he that beholdeth me beholdeth Him that sent me," John 12:44, 45. He alone is the true Revealer of God to men. "All things have been delivered unto me of my Father: and no one knoweth the Son save the Father; neither doth any know the Father save the Son, and he to whomsoever the Son willeth to reveal Him," Matt. 11:27. In the parable of the wicked husbandmen Jesus presents Himself as the Son and Heir of the vineyard, occupying a category higher than that of the prophets, who was rejected and slain,

Christ's Own Testimony Concerning His Deity 13

but who eventually is to be made "the head of the corner," Matt. 21:33-45. His activity is co-extensive with that of the Father: "For what things soever He doeth, these the Son also doeth in like manner," John 5:19, — a joint activity which from other sources we learn extends even to the resurrection and the judgment.

That Jesus' claim to Sonship and to oneness with the Father was understood by the Jews to imply Diety is quite clear. When on one occasion they took up stones to stone Him, He said, "Many good works have I showed you from the Father; for which of those works do ye stone me?", they replied, "For a good work we stone thee not, but for blasphemy; and because that thou, being a man, makest thyself God,"John 10:32, 33. And when they accused Him before Pilate they said: "We have a law, and by that law He ought to die, because He made Himself the Son of God," John 19:7.

The last words of Jesus to His disciples as recorded in John, chapters 14 to 16, are the words of God to men. For a mere man to speak to other men as He speaks here would be blasphemy. He begins by exhorting his disciples to have the same faith in Him that they have in God: "Believe in God, believe also in me." He declares that He goes to heaven to prepare a place for them, and that He will come again and receive them. He declares that He is the way, the truth, and the life, and that no one comes unto the Father except through Him. To know Him is to know the Father, and to see Him, is to see the Father, for He and the Father are one. He goes to the Father, and promises that all of their prayers made in His name shall be answered. He promises to send them the Holy Spirit, another Divine Person, who is to take His place as their Comforter and Companion and Teacher, who is to be to them what He has been and to do for them what He has done, who is to render them infallible as teachers, and who is to give spiritual illumination to all believers. He declares that He is the true source of life to the Church, and that it is as necessary that every believer be united with Him as it is that the branch be united with the vine. They have not chosen Him but He has chosen them, with the result that such a tremendous gulf has been placed between them and "the world" that the world no longer recognizes them as of its kind and therefore hates them. He who hates Him hates His Father also. All things whatsoever the Father has are His, and everything asked in His name will be granted. He came out from the Father into the world, and now He is to leave the world and go back to the Father.

In the intercessory prayer He prays that the Father may glorify the Son in order that the Son may glorify the Father. He claims authority to give eternal life to all those whom the Father has given Him, which life consists in knowing God and Himself. He prays that the Father may glorify Him with the Father's own glory, which glory He had with the Father before the world was. He claims that the true disciples have been given to Him by the Father, that He is not of the world, and that He and the Father are one.

During the trial before the Sanhedrin Jesus publicly and explicitly claimed diety and was condemned to death on the charge that He had spoken "blasphemy." In answer to the high priest's question, "Art thou the Christ, the Son of the Blessed?" (or, as Matthew says, "the Son of God"), Jesus replied, "I am: and ye shall see the Son of man sitting at the right hand of Power, and coming with the clouds of heaven." And then we are told that "the high priest rent his clothes, and saith, What further need have we of witnesses? Ye have heard the blasphemy: what think ye? And they all condemned Him to be worthy of death," Mark 14:61-64.

Christ's Own Testimony Concerning His Deity 15

In giving the Great Commission to the disciples Jesus said: "All authority hath been given unto me in heaven and on earth. Go ye therefore, and make disciples of all the nations, baptizing them in the name of the Father and of the Son and of the Holy Spirit: teaching them to observe all things whatsoever I commanded you: and lo, I am with you always, even unto the end of the world," Matt. 28:18-20. There He placed His name at the center of the triune name of God, commanded that those who believe on Him should be baptized in that name, and promised to be with them always, even unto the end of the world. Concerning this Dr. Benjamin B. Warfield says: "Claiming for Himself all authority in heaven and on earth — which implies the possession of omnipotence — and promising to be with His followers 'always, even unto the end of the world' — which adds the implications of omnipresence and omniscience — He commands them to baptize their converts 'in the name of the Father and of the Son and of the Holy Spirit.' The precise form of the formula must be carefully observed. It does not read: 'In the names' (plural) — as if there were three beings enumerated, each with its distinguishing name. Nor yet: 'In the name of the Father, Son and Holy Spirit,' as if there were one person, going by a threefold name. It reads: 'In the name (singular) of the Father and of the (article repeated) Son, and of the (article repeated) Holy Spirit,' carefully distinguishing three persons, though uniting them all under one name. The name of God was to the Jews Jehovah, and to name the name of Jehovah upon them was to make them His. What Jesus did in this great injunction was to command His followers to name the name of God upon their converts, and to announce the name of God which is to be named on their converts in the threefold enumeration of 'the Father' and 'the Son' and 'the Holy Spirit.' As it is unquestionable that He here intended Himself by 'the Son,' He here places Himself by the side of the Father and the Spirit, as together with them constituting the one God. It is, of course, the Trinity which he is describing; and that is as much as to say that He announces Himself as one of the persons of the Trinity."[1]

Certainly on the basis of His own teaching Jesus claimed Deity for Himself. No unprejudiced reader can reach any other conclusion. Such has been the impression of the great mass of those who have read the New Testament. This has led Dr. A. H. Strong to observe that "If He is not God, He is a deceiver or is self-deceived, and in either case, *Christ, if not God, is not good.*" And Dr. E. Y. Mullins has pointed out that if we deny His Deity then "we must conclude that, with all His moral beauty and excellence, Jesus was a pitiable failure as teacher if He did not succeed in guarding His message against corruptions which have led to His own exaltation as God, and to the existence through eighteen centuries of a system of idolatry of which He is the center."

---

1. *Biblical Doctrines,* p. 204.

III.

TESTIMONY OF THE APOSTLES

IN FULL harmony with the claims and testimony of Jesus concerning His Deity are those of all of the others who speak in the New Testament. The angel Gabriel in announcing to Zacharias that he and Elizabeth were to have a son said that the mission of that son would be "to make ready for the Lord a people prepared for Him," Luke 1:17; and in announcing to Mary that she was to be the mother of a Son who without any human father was to be conceived through the power of the Holy Spirit he said: "He shall be great, and shall be called the Son of the Most High: and the Lord God shall give unto Him the throne of His father David: and He shall reign over the house of Jacob for ever; and of His kingdom there shall be no end," Luke 1:32, 33,—qualifications which can be met by no one who is less than Deity. His name was to be called "Jesus," "for it is He that shall save His people from their sins," Matt. 1:21,—again a work which can be performed by no one who is less than Deity. Matthew, citing one of the Messianic prophecies in the Old Testament, says: "Now all this is come to pass, that it might be fulfilled which was spoken by the Lord through the prophet, saying, Behold, the virgin shall be with child, and shall bring forth a son, And they shall call His name Immanuel; which is, being interpreted, God with us," 1:22, 23. The wise-men, finding the new-born babe after their long journey from the east and possessing a spiritual insight above that commonly given to men, "fell down and worshipped him," Matt. 2:11,—thereby rendering to Him the homage which it is idolatrous and sinful to render to any one other than Deity.

John the Baptist, stern preacher of righteousness that he was, acknowledged himself to be only the fore-runner of one who was coming later and declared that this one was so much greater than he that he was not even worthy to unloose the latchet of His shoes,—that is, not even worthy to be His servant. When Jesus did appear and was baptized John saw the heavens opened and the Spirit of God descending upon Him; and the Father's voice spoke from heaven, saying, "This is my beloved Son, in whom I am well pleased," Matt. 3:17. And the following day he pointed out Jesus as "the Lamb of God, that taketh away the sin of the world," as "He that baptizeth in the Holy Spirit," and as "the Son of God," John 1:29-34.

In the prologue of the Gospel of John we have a clear and unmistakable assertion of the Deity of Christ. "In the beginning was the Word, and the Word was with God, and the Word was God" (vs. 1). John applies to Christ a term which is not found anywhere else in the New Testament, and the predicates which he ascribes to Him can be ascribed to none other than full Deity. In our ordinary language a word reveals the idea which is behind it. What a word is to an idea, Christ is to God, that is, a Revealer. It is His office to make God known to His creatures. "No man hath seen God at any time; the only begotten Son, who is in the bosom of the Father, He hath declared Him" (vs. 18). His eternity is set forth by the statement that "in the beginning," when things began to come into existence, He already "was". The imperfect tense sets forth the notion of absolute supra-temporal existence, so that, as Dr. Warfield says, "From all eternity the Word has been with God as a fellow: He who in the very beginning already 'was,' 'was' also in communion with God. Though He was thus in some sense a second along with God, He was nevertheless not a separate being from God: 'And the Word was God.' In some sense distinguishable from God, He was in an equally true sense identical with God. There is but one eternal God; this eternal God, the Word is; in whatever sense we may distinguish Him from the God whom He is 'with,' He is not another than this God, but Himself is this God."[1]

And in John's prologue not only is the Word taken entirely out of the category of creatures and declared to antedate all things; He is declared to be the Creator of all things: "All things were made through Him; and without Him was not anything made that hath been made" (vs. 3). In verse 14 he says: "And the Word became flesh, and dwelt among us (and we beheld His glory, glory as of the only begotten from the Father), full of grace and truth." John would have us realize that this Christ, who in still another connection he says has "come in the flesh," I John 4:2, is not merely God's eternal fellow, but that He is the eternal God Himself, and that even through the veil of His humanity the disciples were able to behold something of His celestial glory. He uses the term "flesh" to indicate human nature in general, with its implications of dependence and weakness. In his prologue then John simply teaches that the eternal God entered upon a mode of existence in which the experiences that are common to human beings would also be His; in short, that He became incarnate in Jesus Christ the man.

Peter doubtless spoke for most of the disciples when in his great confession he said, "Thou art the Christ, the Son of the

---
1. *Biblical Doctrines*, p. 191.

living God," Matt. 16:16. And as the revelation proceeded toward its climax even the most dubious disciple came to the point where he fell down at Jesus' feet with the acknowledgment, "My Lord and my God," John 20:28. Since those words went unrebuked by Jesus they were equivalent to an assertion on His own part of His claim to Deity.

The testimony of the apostles as they wrought miracles in His name is further proof of His deity. "In the name of Jesus Christ of Nazareth, walk," said Peter to the lame man at the door of the temple, Acts 3:6. "If we this day are examined concerning a good deed done to an impotent man," said he, "by what means this man is made whole; be it known to you all, and to all the people of Israel, that in the name of Jesus Christ of Nazareth, whom ye crucified, whom God raised from the dead, even in Him doth this man stand here before you whole," Acts 4:9, 10. And Paul, casting out an evil spirit from a possessed maid, said: "I charge thee in the name of Jesus Christ to come out of her," Acts 16:18. As Stephen was being stoned to death as the first Christian martyr, he gave his testimony: "Behold, I see the heavens opened, and the Son of Man standing on the right hand of God," Acts 7:56.

Paul repeatedly and consistently teaches the Deity of Christ. Immediately after his conversion he went into the synagogues in Damascus and "proclaimed Jesus, that He is the Son of God," Acts 9:20. Writing to the Colossians he set forth Christ as "the image of the invisible God," 1:15, and declared that "In Him dwelleth all the fulness of the Godhead bodily," 2:9,—in other words, that Christ is an incarnation of the Godhead in all its fulness, a form of statement that cannot be harmonized with the view that He is anything less than God. To the Corinthians he wrote that "God was in Christ, reconciling the world unto Himself," II Cor. 5:19.

Writing to the Romans he refers to the Jews as his kinsmen, "of whom," he says, "is Christ as concerning the flesh, who is over all, God blessed for ever," 9:5,—and a scholar and theologian of such unimpeachable authority as Dr. Warfield, translating from the Greek, insists that Paul here calls Christ by the supreme name of "God over all," so that the verse should read, "of whom is Christ as concerning the flesh, who is God over all, blessed for ever."

Exhorting the Philippian Christians to follow the example of Christ in humility and service Paul wrote: "Have this mind in you which was also in Christ Jesus: who, existing in the form of God" (that is, sharing fully in the Divine nature and possessing all of the attributes and qualities that make God what He is) "counted not the being on an equality with God a thing to be grasped" (did not selfishly choose to remain exclusively in that blessed condition while men continued to be the victims of sin and misery), "but emptied Himself, taking the form of a servant, being made in the likeness of men; and being found in fashion as a man, He humbled Himself, becoming obedient even unto death, yea, the death of the cross" (that is, He took into union with His Divine nature a human nature, and that, of course, without losing or modifying His Divine nature, which is perfect and immutable, became incarnate, accepted the conditions of servanthood, and then, as God clothed in human nature, offered Himself as the Substitute for His people. In fulfilling His mission He thus submitted Himself to the prescribed penalty for sin, which is suffering and death). "Wherefore also," says Paul, "God highly exalted Him" (exalted the Divine-human Person, the God-man, since not the Divine nature as such but only the human nature is capable of receiving added glory and honor), "and gave unto Him the name which is above every name; that in the name of Jesus" (the name of the God-man, as God clothed in human nature, who is the object of worship) "every knee should bow, of things on earth and things under the earth, and that every tongue should confess that Jesus Christ is Lord, to the glory of God the Father" (the term "Lord" being used here not merely in the sense in which men are invested with authority or dignity, but in the sense of absolute sovereignty, the New Testament writers often applying to Jesus Old Testament texts in which the term "Lord" in the Hebrew is *Adhonai* or *Jahweh*, translated Jehovah), Phil. 2:5-11.

The writer of the Epistle to the Hebrews ascribes Deity to Christ when he says that God, having spoken in earlier times through the prophets and in other ways, in these later days has spoken unto us "in His Son, whom He appointed Heir of all things, through whom also He made the worlds; who being the effulgence of His glory, and the very image of His substance, and upholding all things by the word of His power, when He had made purification of sins, sat down on the right hand of the Majesty on high," 1:1-3. And when in John's description of the Holy City, the new Jerusalem, we are told that "the city hath no need of the sun, neither of the moon, to shine upon it: for the glory of God did lighten it, and the lamp thereof is the Lamb" (Rev. 21:23), the last two clauses, according to the usual Hebrew parallelism, are synonymous and so teach the Deity of Christ.

The constant assumption of the writers throughout the New Testament as they record the teachings and miracles and promises of Christ is that He claimed to be and was Deity. After the testimony of Christ Himself the most competent witnesses to His Person and work are those who knew Him most intimately. "Ye also bear witness," said He, "because ye have been with me from the beginning," John 15:27. And their faithfulness to their Master is attested by the records of

Testimony of the Apostles

the early Church which tells us that practically all of them sealed their witness with their own life's blood.

Furthermore, the Roman centurion who witnessed the crucifixion adds his testimony: "Truly this man was the Son of God," Mark 15:39. And even the demons, fallen beings who had known Him in a former state of existence, at His command came out of possessed persons, saying, "What have we to do with thee, thou Son of God? art thou come hither to torment us before the time?" Matt. 8:29.

Christ's resurrection from the dead is also an inescapable proof of His Deity. Both His death and His resurrection were within His own power. Concerning His life He said, "No one taketh it away from me, but I lay it down of myself. I have power to lay it down, and I have power to take it again," John 10:18. Repeatedly He predicted His resurrection from the dead: "And the Son of Man shall be delivered unto the chief priests and the scribes; and they shall ... kill Him; and after three days He shall rise again," Mark 10:33, 34; 8:31; 9:31; Luke 18:33; 24:7; Matt. 20.19; 27:63. Paul points to the resurrection as a proof of Deity, saying that thereby He "was declared to be the Son of God with power, according to the spirit of holiness, by the resurrection from the dead," Rom. 1:4. It was this which convinced Thomas, the most dubious of the disciples, so that at the mere sight of Jesus he acknowledged Him as his Lord and His God (John 20:26-29).

IV.

TITLES ASCRIBED TO JESUS CHRIST

THE name "Jesus," meaning "Saviour," was the name given to our Lord in accordance with the directions of the angel to Joseph and Mary: "Thou shalt call His name JESUS; for it is He that shall save His people from their sins," Matt. 1:21; Luke 1:31. It is the Grecianized form of the Hebrew name Joshua, which mean "Jehovah is salvation." It became His personal name, and as such was designed to express the special office that He was to fulfill.

The term "Christ," meaning "anointed," was our Lord's official title, although often used as a proper name. It is from the Greek *Christos*, and corresponds to the Hebrew *Mashiah*, Messiah. The kings of Israel were anointed with oil as a part of their coronation, I Sam. 9:16; 10:1; II Sam. 19:10; and the king was sometimes called "Jehovah's anointed," I Sam. 24:6. The title "Christ" is therefore a reminder that He is a King in the highest sense. And the combined name, Jesus Christ, thus means that He is the anointed Saviour.

The New Testament records make it clear that Jesus accepted from men the loftiest titles, that He permitted men to render to Him and that He received as His just due all that God requires for Himself. He forbade others to be called Rabbi or Master (Matt. 23:8-10), but accepted for Himself the title Rabbi (John 4:31; 9:2), and expressly claimed the titles Teacher and Lord: "Ye call me, Teacher, and, Lord: and ye say well; for so I am," John 13:13. When preparing for the public entry into Jerusalem He sent two of the disciples to bring a colt, and instructed them to say to any one who might question them, "The Lord hath need of him," Mark 11:3.

Throughout the New Testament Christ is called "Lord," not merely in the sense in which men are invested with authority or dignity or ownership, but in the sense of Absolute and Supreme Sovereign, Preserver, Protector. He is Lord to the Christians in precisely the same sense that Jehovah was Lord to the people of the Old Testament. A few examples are: "For there is born to you this day in the city of David a Saviour, who is Christ the Lord," Luke 2:11; "The Son of Man is Lord of the Sabbath," Luke 6:5; "That every tongue should confess that Jesus Christ is Lord, to the glory of God the Father," Phil. 2:11; "The Lord of glory," I Cor. 2:8; "The Lord is at hand," Phil. 4:5; "Have mercy on me, O Lord," Matt. 15:22; "If thou shalt confess with thy mouth Jesus as Lord, and shalt believe in thy heart that God raised Him from the dead, thou shalt be saved," Rom. 10:9. "Preaching good tidings of peace by Jesus Christ (He is Lord of all)," Acts 10:36. "Holy, holy, holy, is the Lord God, the Almighty, who was and who is and who is to come," Rev. 4:8; "Worthy art thou, our Lord and our God, to receive the glory and the power: for thou didst create all things, and because of thy will they were, and were created," Rev. 4:11; "And He hath on His garment and on His thigh a name written, King of Kings, and Lord of Lords," Rev. 19:16. Christ is acknowledged to be the Lord of all, of those who are in heaven and of those who are on the earth. To Him all creatures are to bow and acknowledge His absolute dominion. He has a right in us and an authority over us which belongs only to One who is our Creator and Redeemer.

At the beginning of his letters Paul commonly places an introductory sentence in which the conjunct name, "God our Father and the Lord Jesus Christ," is used as the Christian pariphrasis for "God." (Cp. Rom. 1:7; I Cor. 1:3; II Cor. 1:2; Gal. 1:3; etc.). It is, in fact, a formula designating the Christian's God and setting forth the Father and the Son on a plane of absolute equality. The Father and the Son are thus indissolubly knit together as essentially one; yet they are not identified, for certain activities are ascribed to one which are not shared by the other, as when, for instance, in Gal. 1:1 we read of "Jesus Christ, and God the Father, who raised Him from the dead," and in Gal. 1:3 we read of "God the Father, and our Lord Jesus Christ, who gave Himself for our sins."

In the Apostolic Benediction, "The grace of the Lord Jesus Christ, and the love of God, and the communion of the Holy Spirit, be with you all," II Cor. 13:14, the name of the Lord Jesus Christ is linked on a plane of absolute equality with that of God the Father and the Holy Spirit as the source of all spiritual blessing.

In the New Testament various names which in the Old Testament are applied only to Deity are applied to Christ. In recording the birth of Christ Matthew applies to Him the name Immanuel, saying, "Now all this is come to pass, that it might be fulfilled which was spoken by the Lord through the prophet, saying, Behold, the virgin shall be with child, and shall bring forth a son, And they shall call his name Immanuel; which is, being interpreted, God with us," 1:22, 23; and in Is. 7:14 we read: "Behold, a virgin shall conceive, and bear a son, and shall call his name Immanuel." In the New Testament Christ is constantly set forth as our King and Redeemer and as an eternal personage. Concerning his vision of the exalted and reigning Christ John says,

"And when I saw Him, I fell at His feet as one dead. And He laid His right hand upon me, saying, Fear not; for I am the first and the last, and the Living One; and I was dead, and behold, I am alive for evermore, and I have the keys of death and of hades," Rev. 1:17, 18; and again, "I am the Alpha and the Omega, the first and the last, the beginning and the end," Rev. 22:13; and in Is. 44:6 we read: "Thus saith Jehovah, the King of Israel, and his Redeemer, Jehovah of hosts: I am the first, and I am the last; and besides me there is no God." We have seen that in the New Testament Jesus Christ is repeatedly called Lord. In the Old Testament the predicted Messiah is sometimes called Lord: "Jehovah saith unto my Lord, Sit thou at my right hand, Until I make thine enemies thy footstool," Ps. 110:1 (compare with Matt. 22:44, where Jesus applies this verse to Himself) and in Mal. 3:1 we read: "The Lord, whom ye seek, will suddenly come to His temple."

Dr. Wm. C. Robinson, of Columbia Theological Seminary, has pointed out that "The Greek New Testament directly applies to Jesus the name 'God' some ten or more times (John 1:1, 18 [Aleph B. C. text]; 20:28; I John 5:20; Heb. 1:8; II Peter 1:1; Acts 20:28; Rom. 9:5; II Thess. 1:12; Titus 2:13; and perhaps Acts 18:26; Heb. 19; I Tim. 3:16). And no less significant is the phenomenon, recognized by scholars of widely differing schools, that Jesus is identified by the New Testament writers as the Lord of the Old Testament when they apply to Him Old Testament texts in which the original is written of *Adhonay* or *Jahweh* (Jehovah) (Is. 40:3; Mark 1:3; Joel 2:32; Acts 2:34; Rom. 10:13; Is. 45:23; Phil. 2:10; Jer. 9:24; I Cor. 1:31; 10:17; Ps. 68:18; Eph. 4:8; Is. 2:19; II Thess. 1:9; II Sam. 3:39; II Tim. 4:14; Rev. 22:13)."

It is to be noted, therefore, that in the New Testament Christ is called: "Lord," Phil. 2:11; "Lord of Lords," I Tim. 6:15; "King of Kings," I Tim. 6:15; "The King of Israel," John 1:49; "The Saviour," II Peter 1:1; "Master," Matt. 23:10; Jude 4; "Son of God," John 1:34; 20:31; "Son of Man," Matt. 17:9; "Jesus," Matt. 1:23; "Christ," Matthew 16:16; "Saviour," John 4:42; Acts 5:31; "Messiah," John 1:41; 4:25, 26; "The Lamb of God," John 1:29; "The Word," John 1:1, "The Only Begotten Son," John 3:16; "Redeemer," Gal. 3:13; "The Lord of Glory," I Cor. 2:8; "The Image of God," II Cor. 4:4; "The Effulgence of His Glory," Heb. 1:3; "The Very Image of His Substance," Heb. 1:3; "Great High Priest," Heb. 4:14; "Mediator," Heb. 12:24; "The Author of our Salvation," Heb. 2:10; "The Author and Perfector of our faith," Eph. 5:23; "The Head of the Church," Eph. 5:23; "The Head of every man," I Cor. 11:3; "The Power of God, and the Wisdom of God," I Cor. 1:24; "The Bread of Life," John 6:35; "The Living Bread," John 6:51; "The True Vine," John 15:1; "The Door," John 10:7; "The Holy and Righteous One," Acts 3:14; "The Prince of Life," Acts 3:15; "God blessed for ever," Rom. 9:5; "The Alpha and the Omega," Rev. 21:6; "The Beginning and the End," Rev. 21:6; "The First and the Last," Rev. 1:17; "The Living One," Rev. 1:18; "The Lord God," Rev. 1:8; "My Lord and My God," John 20:28; "The One who is and who was and who is to come," Rev. 1:8; "The Almighty," Rev. 1:8; "The Holy One of God," John 6:69; "The One through whom the world was made," John 1:2, 10; "The Heir of all things," Heb. 1:2. He thus accepted from men the loftiest titles, the most exalted honor, and the most absolute devotion. No one other than God could have allowed such titles to have gone unrebuked, or indeed have sought after or applied them to Himself.

Two of these titles, "Son of God," and "Son of Man," require more extended treatment and we shall take them up in the following sections.

V.

THE SON OF GOD

ONE OF the most exalted titles applied to Jesus is that of "The Son of God." It is a divine title or name which calls attention to the dignity of His Person, particularly to His Deity, and indicates that He is fully qualified to speak to men concerning the things of God. It was this side of His nature that impressed Nathaniel when, amazed at Jesus' familiarity with his past life, he exclaimed, "Rabbi, thou art the Son of God; thou art King of Israel," John 1:49. It was against this side of His nature that the Devil attempted to throw doubt when he issued the challenge, "If thou art the Son of God, command that these stones become bread," and, "If thou art the Son of God, cast thyself down" (from the pinnacle of the temple), Matt. 4:3, 6; and it was also against this side of His nature that the demons cried out when they said, "What have we to do with thee, thou Son of God? art thou come hither to torment us before the time?" Matt. 8:29. Lazarus' death and restoration to life was especially intended "for the glory of God, that the Son of God may be glorified thereby," John 11:4. Peter's great confession, "Thou art the Christ, the Son of the living God," Matt. 16:16, was prompted by his perception of Christ's essential Deity. And John declared specifically that his purpose in writing his Gospel was, "That ye may believe that Jesus is the Christ, the Son of God; and that believing ye may have life in His name," 20:31.

In connection with an earlier treatment of the doctrine of the Trinity we have pointed out that in theological language the terms "Father" and "Son" carry with them not our occidental ideas of, on the one hand, source of being and superiority, and on the other, subordination and dependence, but rather the Semitic and oriental ideas of *likeness* or *sameness of nature* and equality of being. It is, of course, the Semitic consciousness that underlies the phraseology of Scripture, and wherever the Scriptures call Christ the "Son of God" they assert His true and proper Deity. It signifies a unique relationship that cannot be predicated of nor shared with any creature. As any merely human son is like his father in his essential nature, that is, possessed of humanity, so Christ, the Son of God, was like His Father in His essential nature, that is, possessed of Deity. The Father and the Son, together with the Holy Spirit, are co-eternal and co-equal in power and glory, and partake of the same nature or substance. They have always existed as distinct Persons. The Father is, and always has been, as much dependent on the Son as the Son is on the Father; for self-existence and independence are properties not of the Persons within the Godhead but of the Triune God. Consequently, the terms "Father" and "Son" are not at all adequate to express the full relationship which exists between the first and second Persons of the Godhead. But they are the best we have. Moreover, they are the terms used in Scripture, and besides expressing the ideas of sameness of nature they are found to be reciprocal, expressing the ideas of love, affection, trust, honor, unity and harmony, — ideas of endearment and preciousness.

Christ is the Son of God by nature; we become the sons of God by grace. He is the Son of God in His own right; we become sons of God by adoption. He has existed thus from eternity; we become sons in time as we are regenerated to a new life and have His righteousness imparted to us. This, of course, does not mean that we ever come to partake of the nature of Deity. But it does mean that we have restored to us and perfected in us that moral and spiritual likeness of God with which we were created but which became lost through sin. God is the Father of the Lord Jesus Christ in a sense in which He is the Father of none other. Jesus did, indeed, speak to the disciples about "your Father who is in heaven," but in so doing He made it clear that the term was used only in a contingent sense. Their sonship with God came through Him and was dependent on their relation with Him: "The Father Himself loveth you, because ye have loved me, and have believed that I came forth from the Father," John 16:27; or as John so beautifully points out in another place, "As many as received Him, to them gave He the right to become the sons of God; even to them that believe on His name," 1:12.

The Scriptures do not teach a doctrine of the universal fatherhood of God and the universal brotherhood of men. That is one of the doctrines of present-day Modernism. The Scriptures teach, not a sonship based on the natural relationship which God bears to all men because of creation, but a sonship based on a spiritual re-creation, a sonship into which man comes through faith in Christ. In the broad sense it is, of course, true that God is the Father of all men since He has created them; but in a narrower and far more important sense He is the Father only of those who have been regenerated and who are therefore "in Christ" in such a sense that to some extent they partake of His holiness, those who have been "born anew" (John 3:3). "If any man is in Christ, he is a new creature," Paul wrote to the Corinthians, II Cor. 5:17. And to the Romans he wrote: "As many as are led by the Spirit of God, these are sons of God," 8:14. All true Christians are "sons of God, through faith, in Christ

Jesus," Gal. 3:26. "If ye are Christ's, then are ye Abraham's seed," and therefore "heirs according to promise," Gal. 3:29. Outside of the sphere of redemption the term "Father" can have only a very shallow meaning; for it is only through Christ that we can really know God: "Neither doth any know the Father, save the Son, and he to whomsoever the Son willeth to reveal Him," Matt. 11:37. Those who are still in sin, fallen, unregenerate worldlings, are said to be not sons of God but *sons of the Devil,* because basically and in principle they are like the Devil and partake of his evil nature. They are "by nature children of wrath," Eph. 2:3. To His opponents Jesus said, "Ye are of your father the Devil, and the lusts of your father it is your will to do," John 8:44; and again, "I speak the things which I have seen with my Father: and ye also do the things which ye have heard from your father. . . . . If God were your Father, ye would love me: for I came forth and am come from God," John 8:38, 42. Paul teaches this same truth. To Elymas the sorcerer he said: "O full of all guile and all villainy, thou son of the Devil, thou enemy of all righteousness, wilt thou not cease to pervert the right way of the Lord," Acts 13:10.

God is Father primarily because of the relationship which He sustains to Christ the Son; and only as we are spiritually united to Christ do we become children of God. He has "foreordained us unto adoption as sons through Jesus Christ unto Himself," Eph. 1:5. Christ was the Son of God in such a high sense that He Himself could say, "I and the Father are one," John 10:30; "He that hath seen me hath seen the Father," John 14:9; "He that honoreth not the Son honoreth not the Father," 5:23; that Paul could say that He is "the image of the invisible God," Col. 1:15; that "God was in Christ reconciling the world unto Himself," II, 5:19; that "In Him dwelleth all the fulness of the Godhead bodily," Col. 2:9;

and that the writer of the Epistle to the Hebrews could say that He is "the effulgence of His glory, and the very image of His substance," 1:3. The recorded discourses of Jesus make it perfectly clear that He was continually conscious of His Deity, that He was the Son of God in a unique sense, gazing unbrokenly into the depths of the Divine Being, knowing the Father fully even as He was known of the Father.

That the terms "Father" and "Son" as used by Jesus and as understood by His hearers carried with them the claim to equality and identity is made clear by the response of the Jews. When after healing a man on the Sabbath Jesus said to them, "My Father worketh even until now, and I work," we are told that "The Jews sought the more to kill Him, because He not only brake the Sabbath, but also called God His own Father, making Himself equal with God," John 5:17, 19. And a little later they said, "For a good work we stone thee not, but for blasphemy; and because that thou, being a man, makest thyself God," John 10:33. It was specifically for claiming to be "the Christ, the Son of God," that He was accused of blasphemy by the high priest and sentenced to death by the Sanhedrin (Matt. 26:63-66). "We have a law, and by that law He ought to die, because He made Himself the Son of God," said the Jews, John 19:7. And Jesus did not deny, but acknowledged, the accuracy of their charge. If they had been wrong a word from Him would have set them right, and it would have been nothing short of criminal for Him to have withheld it. But certainly He did not go to His death "for a metaphor," as some one has expressed it. It was not because of a slight misunderstanding of His claims that He allowed Himself to be murdered by His enemies, but because His claims were accurately understood and insisted upon that He went to the cross.

From John Calvin comes the following useful observation concerning the title, "Son of God": "As He has received from His mother that which causes Him to be called the Son of David, so He has from His Father that which constitutes Him the Son of God, and this is something distinct and different from His humanity. The Scriptures distinguish Him by two names, calling Him sometimes 'The Son of God,' sometimes 'the Son of Man.' With respect to the latter, it cannot be disputed that He is styled the 'Son of Man,' in conformity to the common idiom of the Hebrew language, because He is one of the posterity of Adam. I contend, on the other hand, that He is denominated 'the Son of God' on account of His Deity and eternal existence; because it is equally reasonable that the appelation of 'Son of God' should be referred to the Divine nature, as that that of 'Son of Man' should be referred to the human nature."[1]

It is thus abundantly clear that the name "Son of God" was designed to set forth Christ in His essential nature as Deity. He who was "born of the seed of David according to the flesh" is also "declared to be the Son of God with power," Rom. 1:3, 4; and He who "as concerning the flesh" came of the Jews is also declared to be "over all, God blessed for ever," Rom. 9:5. We are, therefore, to believe in the Son as we do in the Father, and to honor the one as we do the other.

---
1. *The Institutes*, Vol. I, p. 442.

VI.

THE SON OF MAN

THE title that Jesus most often used when speaking of Himself, and which therefore appears to have been His favorite title, was, "Son of Man." This much discussed title, whatever else it may mean, certainly was designed to call attention to the fact that He possessed real humanity. He is the representative man. We can point to Him and say, There is real manhood. In Him human nature is seen at its perfection, functioning as was intended when it left the hands of the Creator. He is the ideal after whom all others should pattern their lives. And since He thus possessed human nature in His own Person, He is vitally related to all other members of the human race and, by Divine appointment, is capable of acting as their representative before God.

In the eighth Psalm this title is used with reference to mankind in general: "What is man, that thou art mindful of him? And the son of man, that thou visitest him?" But as applied to Jesus in the New Testament it had more than human connotations. It went back to the heavenly figure in Daniel 7:13, 14, where, prophetic of the return of Christ to heaven after the completion of His work of redemption, "there came with the clouds of heaven one like unto a Son of Man, and He came even to the Ancient of Days, and they brought Him near before Him. And there was given Him dominion, and glory, and a kingdom, that all peoples, nations, and languages should serve Him: His dominion is an everlasting dominion, which shall not pass away, and His kingdom that which shall not be destroyed." To Jewish ears, therefore, it was a clear assertion of Messiahship. And that Jesus used it with full consciousness of its significance is very evident, for He Himself said: "Then shall appear the sign of the Son of Man in heaven: and then shall all the tribes of the earth mourn, and they shall see the Son of Man coming on the clouds of heaven with power and great glory. And He shall send forth His angels with a great sound of a trumpet, and they shall gather together His elect from the four winds, from one end of heaven to the other," Matt. 24:30, 31. And in the parallel passage in Luke He says, "Even so ye also, when ye see these things coming to pass, know ye that the *kingdom of God* is nigh," 21:31.

Some New Testament scholars have called the name "Son of Man" the "most celestial" of all of Jesus' titles. The Rev. Leonard Verduin, of the Christian Reformed Church, has thrown a great deal of light on its meaning in the following paragraphs. Says he:

"The name 'Son of Man' has its origin in the heavenlies. It harks back to that supersensitive region where the Council of Redemption met. The name finds its origin in that great conference and in the subject about which it met. At that Conference, as we know, the several persons of the Holy Trinity met to discuss redemption and to draw up a redemption program. Redemption strategy was determined upon. And since the proposed program of salvation for mortal men required the incarnation of Deity it had to be determined upon which of the three persons this task logically devolved. And for it the Son was indicated. Not the Father, nor the Spirit, but the Son was to be made after the fashion of men. He was to become very man, become such by assuming human nature, by becoming 'Son of Man' in a word. And that appelation became the exclusive property of the Son henceforth. This gives us the necessary background to any fair evaluation of the name 'Son of Man.' Needless to say, a generation of thinkers that is quite careless concerning the momentous doctrine of Christ's pre-existence has by its very bias of unbelief insulated itself against a proper appreciation of the name 'Son of Man.' "

"Now by common consent names are chosen to draw attention to that which is unique in the bearer. A boy with unusually red hair will likely be called 'Red' or 'Sandy.' If he is unusually tall he will soon be called 'Slim,' etc. Men are not named for that which is common but for that which is unique, uncommon. And in the mind of the eternal Son of God His own uniqueness lay not in His Deity—that He had in common with the Father and the Spirit. With them He shared His ubiquity, His eternity, His omniscience, etc. But the prospect of incarnation was His and His alone. Therein lay His uniqueness in the divine economy. Is it any wonder that in that heavenly society the name 'Son of Man' was invented and applied to this prospective visitor to earth and earth-men?"[1]

It should be observed further that since the term "Son of Man" was invented in connection with His proposed visit to earth Jesus quite often uses it when speaking of His coming, or going, or coming again. "The Son of Man came to seek and to save that which was lost," Luke 19:10. "The Son of Man goeth, even as it is written of Him," Matt. 26:24. "What then if ye should behold the Son of Man ascending where He was before?" John 6:62. "In an hour that ye think not the Son of Man cometh," Matt. 24:44. "When the Son of Man shall come in His glory, and all the angels with Him," Matt. 25:31. It has very appropriately been called a "transition" name, and it thus serves not only as a reminder of His union with mankind but also of His higher origin.

---
1. Article in *The Calvin Forum*, Dec. 1940.

VII.

THE PRE-EXISTENCE OF CHRIST

IN A rather remarkable series of statements Jesus conveys to our minds the idea that His existence did not merely begin when He was born in Bethlehem, but that He "came" or "descended" from heaven to earth, or that He was "sent" by the Father. Very evidently if He came or descended or was sent He must have existed before He came or descended or was sent. These verses afford not only a unique testimony to His divine mission, but also to His heavenly origin, and set Him forth not only as the greatest of the sons of men but as a pre-existent Person,—in some instances as an eternal Being. Unquestionably these sayings are spoken out of a consciousness of pre-existence, and cannot be fully satisfied by any other supplement than "from heaven," or "from the Father." And particularly is this true when the title, "Son of Man" (which, as we have just seen in the preceding section, itself implies pre-existence), is used in these verses. He thus sets Himself forth as of higher than human or earthly origin, and therefore a One uniquely qualified to speak to men concerning spiritual things.

Typical verses of this kind are as follows: "The Son of Man came to seek and to save that which was lost," Luke 19:10. "The Son of Man came not to be ministered unto, but to minister, and to give His life a ransom for many," Mark 10:45. "Think not that I came to destroy the law or the prophets: I came not to destroy, but to fulfil," Matt. 5:17. "Let us go elsewhere into the next towns, that I may preach there also; for to this end came I forth," Mark 1:38.

"I was not sent but unto the lost sheep of the house of Israel," Matt. 15:24. "They that are whole have no need of a physician, but they that are sick: I came not to call the righteous, but sinners," Mark 2:17. "Think not that I came to send peace on the earth: I came not to send peace, but a sword. For I am come to set a man at variance against his father, and the daughter against her mother, and the daughter-in-law against her mother-in-law: and a man's foes shall be they of his own household," Matt. 10:34-36 (meaning, of course, not that the ultimate and final purpose of His coming is to stir up strife, but that when the Gospel is preached in a sinful world the first reaction is one of strife with the opposing sinful environment, and that this opposition often disrupts even the most intimate family ties). "I came out from the Father, and am come into the world: again, I leave the world, and go unto the father," John 16:28. "I know whence I came, and whither I go; but ye know not whence I came, or whither I go. . . . I am not alone, but I and the Father that sent me," John 8:14, 16. "Ye are from beneath; I am from above: ye are of this world; I am not of this world," John 8:23. "He that cometh from above is above all: he that is of the earth is of the earth, and of the earth he speaketh: He that cometh from heaven is above all. What He hath seen and heard, of that He beareth witness... He whom God hath sent speaketh the words of God," John 3:31-34. "No one hath ascended into heaven, but He that descended out of heaven, even the Son of Man, who is in heaven," John 3:13. "What then if ye should behold the Son of man ascending where He was before?" John 6:62.

Furthermore, Jesus teaches not only that He existed before coming into the world, but that He has existed from eternity. "And now, Father, glorify thou me with thine own self with the glory which I had with thee before the world

The Pre-Existence of Christ

was," John 17:5. "For thou (Father) lovedst me before the foundation of the world," John 17:24. "Before Abraham was born, I am," John 8:58,—a statement which infers that the ground of His existence is within Himself, and which also is reminiscent of the "I Am That I am," the name by which Jehovah announced Himself to Moses in the wilderness as the self-existent, eternal God. In fact, Jesus here applies to Himself the name which since the time of Moses had been known as the name of the eternal God. And in the book of Revelation the risen and glorified Christ says of Himself, "I am the Alpha and the Omega, the first and the last, the beginning and the end," 22:13.

Thus in explicit terms Jesus teaches not only His pre-existence but His eternal, pre-existence. And with this agree the other witnesses who speak in the New Testament. "After me cometh a man who is become before me: for He was before me," said His forerunner, John the Baptist, John 1:30,—not that Jesus was born earlier than John the Baptist, but that He existed earlier, and therefore stands before him in rank. We have already had occasion to refer to the Prologue of John's Gospel, where concerning the pre-incarnate Word he declares that He possessed not only pre-existence but co-eternity and co-creatorship with the Father, that in time this Word "became flesh and dwelt among us, and we beheld His glory, glory as of the only begotten from the Father, full of grace and truth."

Setting it forth as one of the maxims of fundamental religious truth, Paul says, "Faithful is the saying, and worthy of all acceptation, that Christ Jesus came into the world to save sinners," I Tim. 1:15. Writing to the Colossians he says, "In Him were all things created, in the heavens and upon the earth, things visible and things invisible, whether thrones or dominions or principalities or powers; all things have been created through Him, and unto Him; and He is before all things, and in Him all things consist," 1:16, 17. In I Tim. 3:16 pre-existence is assumed when he refers to Christ as "He who was manifested in the flesh."

The writer of the Epistle to the Hebrews says, "Jesus Christ is the same yesterday and today, yea and for ever," 13:2,—the same through every change and chance of life, the same to this generation that He has been to any past generation. And because He is thus unalterably constant, He is set forth as the Christian's support and stay, the eternal refuge of His people.

Moreover, even the Old Testament predictions in regard to the Messiah who was to come set Him forth not merely as one who would be "born" like other men, but as One who existed before He came to earth, in fact, as One whose existence extends back into eternity. The prophet Micah wrote, "But thou, Bethlehem, Ephrathah, which art little to be among the thousands of Judah, out of thee shall one come forth unto me that is to be ruler in Israel; whose goings forth are from of old, from everlasting," 5:2. And Isaiah described the promised Messiah not only as the "Wonderful Counsellor" and "Prince of Peace," but as the "Mighty God" and as the "Everlasting Father," 9:6.

In all the history of the world Jesus emerges as the only "expected" person. No one was looking for such a person as Julius Caesar, or Napoleon, or Washington, or Lincoln to appear at the time and place that they did appear. No other person has had his course foretold or his work laid out for him centuries before he was born. But the coming of the Messiah had been predicted for centuries. In fact, the first promise of His coming was given to Adam and Eve soon after their fall into sin. As time went on various details concerning His Person and work were revealed through the prophets; and at the time Jesus was born there was a general expectation throughout the Jewish world that the Messiah was soon to appear, even the manner of His birth and the town in which it would occur having been clearly indicated.

Thus Jesus is consistently presented as one who existed before He came to earth. He is presented as One who "descended" from heaven to earth, as One who from all eternity has shared the Father's glory,—in fact, as One who "came out from the Father" (John 16:28) and who was in the most intimate way identified with God. His own words make it clear that He presented Himself as a visitant from a higher sphere, and that He thought of His work on earth as a mission on behalf of men,—in brief, that He came with the explicit purpose of saving the "lost."

It is quite evident that the doctrine of the pre-existence of Christ is a vital factor in any proper understanding of His Person. As Dr. Samuel G. Craig has pointed out, "In our study of Jesus Christ it is of the utmost importance that we interpret His life in the light of His pre-existence. It is important, in the first place, in order that we may keep constantly before us the fact that the Incarnation was not simply the birth of a great man but rather the entering into human conditions of the only-begotten Son of God, and hence that we may ever realize that in Jesus Christ we are face to face with the God-man. It is important, in the second place, in order that we may adequately appreciate the service He has rendered for us. It is simply impossible adequately to appreciate what Jesus has done for us unless we remember that the Son of Man *came* not to be ministered unto but to minister and to give His life a ransom for many."[1]

---
1. *Jesus As He Was And Is*, p. 58.

VIII.

THE ATTRIBUTES OF DEITY ARE ASCRIBED TO CHRIST

THROUGHOUT the New Testament we find that the attributes of Deity are repeatedly ascribed to Christ, and that not merely in a secondary sense such as might be predicated of a creature but in such a sense as is applicable to God alone. The following attributes are ascribed to Him:

1. HOLINESS: "Thou art the Holy One of God," John 6:69. Peter affirms that He "did no sin, neither was guile found in His mouth," I Peter 2:22. Paul refers to Him as "Him who knew no sin," II Cor. 5:21. He was "holy, guileless, undefiled, separate from sinners," says the writer of the Epistle to the Hebrews, 7:26. "I do always the things that are pleasing to Him," said Jesus, John 8:29. "Which of you convicteth me of sin?" was His challenge to His enemies, John 8:46. Even the demons bore witness that He was "the Holy One of God," Luke 4:34.

2. ETERNITY: "In the beginning was the Word," John 1:1. "Before Abraham was born, I am," John 8:58. "The glory which I had with thee (the Father) before the world was," John 17:5. "Thou (Father) lovedst me before the foundation of the world," John 17:24. "He is before all things," Col. 1:17. In the Messianic prophecies He is called the "Everlasting Father," Is. 9:6, and is said to be One "whose goings forth are from of old, from everlasting," Micah 5:2. He is indeed the King of the Ages.

The Attributes of Deity are Ascribed to Christ   45

3. LIFE: "In Him was life," John 1:4. "I am the way, and the truth, and the life: no one cometh unto the Father, but by me," John 14:6. "I am the resurrection, and the life," John 11:25. "For as the Father hath life in Himself, even so gave He to the Son also to have life in Himself," John 3:26.

4. IMMUTABILITY: "Jesus Christ is the same yesterday and today, yea and for ever," Heb. 13:8. "They (the heavens) shall perish; but thou continuest. . . . They shall be changed: but thou art the same," Heb. 1:11,12.

5. OMNIPOTENCE: "All authority has been given unto me in heaven and on earth," Matt. 28:18. "All things have been delivered unto me of my Father," Matt. 11:27. "He (God the Father) put all things in subjection under His feet, and gave Him to be head over all things to the Church," Eph. 1:22. "Upholding all things by the word of His power," Heb. 1:3. "The Lord God, who is and who was and who is to come, the Almighty," Rev. 1:8. In Messianic prophecy He is foretold as the "Mighty God," Is. 9;6. He possessed power to restore the dead to life (John 11:43,44; Luke 7:14), and He declares that the final resurrection of all men will be accomplished through His power: "The hour cometh, in which all that are in the tombs shall hear His voice, and shall come forth; they that have done good, unto the resurrection of life; and they that have done evil, unto the resurrection of judgment," John 5:28,29.

6. OMNISCIENCE: "Thou knowest all things," John 16:30. "Jesus knowing their thoughts," Matt. 9:4. "Knew all men . . . knew what was in man," John 2:24. "Jesus knew from the beginning who they were that believed not, and who it was that should betray Him," John 6:64. "Jesus therefore, knowing all the things that were coming upon Him, went

forth," John 18:4. "Christ, in whom are all the treasures of wisdom and knowledge hidden," Col. 2:3. "No one knoweth the Son, save the Father; neither doth any know the Father, save the Son," Matt. 11:27,—a declaration in which Jesus Himself implies that the personality or being of the Son is so great that only God can fully comprehend it, and that the knowledge of the Son is so unlimited that He can know God to perfection; in other words, a declaration that His knowledge is infinite. Certainly the Gospels present Jesus as endowed with absolute and unlimited knowledge and foresight. Concerning this general theme Dr. J. Ritchie Smith has said: "How well He read the heart is illustrated in the case of Nathanael, of the woman of Samaria, of Judas, and of Peter. He foresaw the future, foretold His death, His resurrection, His return. The map of history was unrolled before Him, and He traced the unfoldings of the old economy, the mighty works to be wrought by His disciples, the overthrow of Satan, the triumph of the kingdom of God. Earth and heaven, time and eternity, God and man lay open to His view."[1]

7. OMNIPRESENCE: "The only begotten Son, who is in the bosom of the Father," John 1:18. Here John declares that although Christ became incarnate and lived on earth His communion with the Father nevertheless continues in the most infinite and unmodified form. He not merely "was" with God, but still "is" with Him, in the fullest sense of the eternal relationship intimated in John 1:1. "No one hath ascended into heaven, but He that descended out of heaven, even the Son of Man, who is in heaven," John 3:13. Calvin has remarked concerning this verse that He was "incarnate, but not incarcerated;" and then he adds: "The Son of God

---

1. *Studies in the Gospel of John*, p. 134.

The Attributes of Deity are Ascribed to Christ 47

miraculously descended from heaven, yet in such a manner that He never left heaven; He chose to be miraculously born of the virgin, to live on the earth, and to be suspended from the cross; and yet He never ceased to fill the universe, in the same manner as from the beginning."[2] Christ Himself set forth His omnipresence when He said, "Where two or three are gathered together in my name, there am I in the midst of them," Matt. 18:20; and again, "Lo, I am with you always, even unto the end of the world," Matt. 28:20. Assembled with His disciples on the mount of Olives after His resurrection, He assured them of His continued presence and power and declared that His influence with them would be, not that of a dead teacher, but of a living presence. Being thus everywhere present, He is always accessible, able to guard and comfort His people so that no affliction or suffering but such as He sees to be for their own good can come upon them. And a remarkable fact which appears as we read the New Testament is that after His resurrection His living presence was more real to His disciples than His bodily presence ever had been before His death, their conviction concerning Him then became a conquering power whereas before His death their estimate of Him was always wavering and doubtful. Paul teaches the omnipresence of Christ when he refers to "the fulness of Him that filleth all in all," Eph. 1:23.

8. CREATION: "All things were made through Him: and without Him was not anything made that hath been made," John 1:3. "The world was made through Him," John 1:10. "In Him were all things created, in the heavens and upon the earth, things visible and things invisible, whether thrones or dominions or principalities or powers; all things have been created through Him, and unto Him; and He is before all

---
2. *Institutes*, I, p. 435.

things, and in Him all things consist," Col. 1:16,17. "But of the Son He saith, Thy throne, O God, is for ever and ever. ... Thou, Lord, in the beginning didst lay the foundation of the earth, and the heavens are the works of thy hands," Heb. 1:8,10,—the writer here applies to Christ words which in the Old Testament are spoken concerning Jehovah, and thereby sets forth His Godhead in the most absolute sense. "One Lord, Jesus Christ, through whom are all things," I Cor. 8:6. And the writer of the Epistle to the Hebrews informs us that even now He is "upholding all things by the word of His power," 1:3.

Thus the Scripture writers set forth the relations which Christ sustains to the universe as a whole. While it is true that in Scripture the chief emphasis is thrown on the relations which He bears to us as our Savior, Master, Teacher and Example, which is, of course, the most vital aspect of His work so far as we are concerned, we must not suppose that these relations comprehend His full significance. To limit Him to these is to rob Him of what are no doubt much greater and more important relations to the remainder of the universe. His significance for the entire universe is constantly assumed throughout Scripture, although not frequently mentioned. It is just because He is the Creator and Ruler of the entire universe that He can say, "All authority hath been given unto me in heaven and on earth," and that He is fitted to be the true Saviour and Master and Teacher of men. Concerning this point Dr. Craig has said: "We are told that it is He who created this universe with all that it contains of things visible and invisible, and hence that not only the physical universe with its myriads of suns and stars but that all forms of personal life, including the most potent of angelic beings, whether they be called thrones or dominions or principalities or powers, as well as men, are indebted to Him for their existence. He is imminent in the universe today, upholding it by His power and preserving it in unity so that it remains a cosmos and does not become a chaos. Finally we are told that as all things visible and invisible, had their source in Him so they move toward Him as their final goal. Not only were all things created 'through Him,' they were also created 'unto Him,' so that He is the last as well as the first, the end as well as the beginning."[3]

9. AUTHORITY TO FORGIVE SINS: "And Jesus seeing their faith saith unto the sick of the palsy, Son, thy sins are forgiven,"—and when some of the scribes, pointedly conscious that this prerogative belongs to God alone, reasoned inwardly, saying, "Why doth this man thus speak? He blasphemeth: who can forgive sins but one, even God?" Jesus said unto them, "That ye may know that the Son of Man hath power on earth to forgive sins (He saith to the sick of the palsy), I say unto thee, Arise, take up thy bed, and go unto thy house. And he arose, and straightway took up his bed, and went forth before them all," Mark 2:5-12. In instituting the Lord's Supper Jesus made it plain that the "remission of sins" was to be accomplished through His shed blood, Matt. 26:28. Not only does He calmly assume the authority to forgive sin in others, but asserts that in His own person and as their substitute He bears the penalty of sin for them. After His resurrection He declared to the disciples that "repentance and remission of sins should be preached in His name unto all the nations," Luke 24:47. John the Baptist bore witness to Him as "the Lamb of God, that taketh away the sin of the world," John 1:29. Peter declares that "every one that believeth on Him shall receive remission of sins," Acts 10:43.

---
3. *Jesus As He Was and Is*, p. 249.

Paul refers to Him as "the Son of His love; in whom we have our redemption, the forgiveness of our sins," Col. 1:14. And John declares that "the blood of Jesus His Son cleanseth us from all sin," I John 1:7. He could forgive the sins of others because He Himself was to pay the price of that absolution.

To assume the authority to forgive sins is to assume one of the prerogatives of God. And to assume that authority unjustly is, of course, a very heinous offense. This, Paul tells us, is the offense of "the man of sin," "the son of perdition," who, he adds, "opposeth and exalteth himself against all that is called God or that is worshipped; so that he sitteth in the temple of God, setting himself forth as God," II Thess. 2:3,4. But Christ claims this authority, and in doing so very definitely sets Himself forth as God. It is interesting to note just here that the Unitarians, who place a disproportionate emphasis on Christ's example to the detriment of His saviourhood, refuse to follow His example when He sets Himself over against His disciples and all others as the One who forgives sins.

10. THE AUTHOR OF SALVATION; THE OBJECT OF FAITH: "He that believeth on the Son hath eternal life; but he that obeyeth not the Son shall not see life, but the wrath of God abideth on him," John 3:36. "Believe on the Lord Jesus, and thou shalt be saved," Acts 16:31. "Believe in God, believe also in me," John 14:1. "For God so loved the world, that He gave His only begotten Son, that whosoever believeth on Him should not perish, but have eternal life. . . . He that believeth on Him is not judged: he that believeth not is judged already, because he hath not believed on the name of the only begotten Son of God," John 3:16,18. "I am the resurrection, and the life: he that believeth on me, though he die, yet shall he live; and whosoever liveth and believeth on

The Attributes of Deity are Ascribed to Christ 51

me shall never die," John 11:26. Faith in Christ is involved in, and in fact is declared to be identical with, faith in God: "And Jesus cried and said, He that believeth on me, believeth not on me, but on Him that sent me. And He that beholdeth me beholdeth Him that sent me," John 12:44,45. "They said therefore unto Him, What must we do that we may work the works of God? Jesus answered and said unto them, This is the work of God, that ye believe on Him whom He hath sent. . . . I am the bread of life: he that cometh unto me shall not hunger, and he that believeth on me shall never thirst. . . . This is the will of my Father, that every one that beholdeth the Son, and believeth on Him, should have eternal life; and I will raise him up at the last day," John 6:28-40. "I am the vine, ye are the branches: he that abideth in me, and I in him, the same beareth much fruit: for apart from me ye can do nothing. If a man abide not in me, he is cast forth as a branch, and is withered; and they gather them, and cast them into the fire, and they are burned," John 15:5,6. "I am the door; by me if any man enter in, he shall be saved," John 10:9. "My sheep hear my voice, and I know them, and they follow me: and I give unto them eternal life," John 10:27,28. "And this is life eternal, that they should know thee the only true God, and Him whom thou didst send, even Jesus Christ," John 17:3. "Come unto me, all ye that labor and are heavy laden, and I will give you rest," Matt. 11:28. "Be thou faithful unto death, and I will give thee the crown of life," Rev. 2:10. "And in none other is there salvation: for neither is there any other name under heaven, that is given among men, wherein we must be saved," Acts 4:12. "No one knoweth the Son, save the Father; neither doth any know the Father, save the Son, and he whomsoever the Son willeth to reveal Him," Matt. 11:27. "Every one therefore who shall confess me before men, him will I also confess before my Father who is in heaven. But whosoever shall deny me before men, him will I also deny before my Father who is in heaven," Matt. 10:32. "Except ye believe that I am He, ye shall die in your sins," John 8:24. Even the name "Jesus" is not of human but of divine origin, and is the equivalent of the Hebrew "Joshua," meaning "Saviour." Even before He came into the world the purpose of His mission was thus designated: "And thou shalt call His name Jesus; for it is He that shall save His people from their sins," Matt. 1:21. And near the close of his Gospel the Apostle John states specifically his purpose in writing: "These (things) are written that ye may believe that Jesus is the Christ, the Son of God; and that believing ye may have life in His name," John 20:31.

These are indeed exceedingly great and precious promises. Certainly they make clear that faith in Christ is necessary for salvation, and that apart from Him there is no salvation. It is impossible for any one to make more stupendous claims than Jesus makes concerning His own Person and His influence over the lives of others. As Dr. Charles Hodge has said, "It is obvious that the infinite God Himself can neither promise nor give anything greater or higher than Christ gives to His people. To Him they are taught to look as the source of all blessing, the giver of every good and perfect gift. There is no more comprehensive prayer in the New Testament than that with which Paul closes his epistle to the Galatians: 'The grace of our Lord Jesus Christ be with your spirit.' His favor is our life, which it could not be if He were not our God."[4]

11. PRAYER AND WORSHIP ARE ASCRIBED TO JESUS: It is universally acknowledged that God alone can hear and

---

[4]. *Systematic Theology*, I, p. 503.

The Attributes of Deity are Ascribed to Christ 53

answer prayer, and that the worship of anything less than Deity is idolatry. Yet Jesus repeatedly sets Himself forth not only as the Revealer of God but as the object of worship. "Whatsoever ye shall ask in my name, that will I do," John 14:13. "If ye shall ask anything of the Father, He will give it you in my name. Hitherto ye have asked nothing in my name: ask, and ye shall receive, that your joy may be made full," John 16:23,24. We read that on numerous occasions Jesus did receive worship while on earth. The Wise-men, having been divinely guided to the Christ-child, when they saw Him, "fell down and worshipped Him," Matt. 2:11. After Jesus had come to the disciples walking on the water, "they that were in the boat worshipped Him, saying, Of a truth thou art the Son of God," Matt. 14:33. Concerning the blind man whose sight was restored when he washed in the pool of Siloam it is said, "And he worshipped Him," John 9:38. On another occasion a certain Canannitish woman "came and worshipped Him, saying, Lord, help me," Matt. 15:25. When confronted with the visible proof of Christ's resurrection, "Thomas answered and said unto Him, My Lord and my God," John 20:28,—a direct ascription of Deity to Christ, and since it went unrebuked it was the equivalent of an assertion of Deity on His part. After the resurrection the disciples went into Galilee, to the place where Jesus had appointed them, "And when they saw Him, they worshipped Him," Matt. 28:17. Luke says that at the time of the ascension, "He parted from them, and was carried up into heaven. And they worshipped Him," 24:51,52. It is not His teachings nor the principles that He set forth, but He Himself that is the object of faith in religion. On numerous occasions Jesus accepted such worship as perfectly proper. Never did He reject it as improper or as misdirected. Promising that He will hear and answer prayer, that where two or three are gathered together in His name there He will be in the midst of them, and that He will be with His people always, even unto the end of the world, He laid direct claim to Deity and set Himself forth as the adequate supply of all of the spiritual needs of those who trust in Him.

With these words of Jesus agree, of course, all of the New Testament writers, the apostolic and the post-apostolic Church. Without exception they accord Him the honor and worship that is due to God alone. "That all may honor the Son, even as they honor the Father. He that honoreth not the Son honoreth not the Father that sent Him," said the Apostle John, 5:23. Stephen died, "calling upon the Lord, and saying, Lord Jesus, receive my spirit," Acts 7:59. In answer to the most important question that man can ask, "What must I do to be saved?" Paul replied, "Believe on the Lord Jesus, and thou shalt be saved," Acts 16:31. "Confess with thy mouth Jesus as Lord," Rom. 10:9. "Whosoever shall call upon the name of the Lord shall be saved," Rom. 10:13. "That in the name of Jesus every knee should bow . . . and that every tongue should confess that Jesus Christ is Lord, to the glory of God the Father," Phil. 2:10,11. "Let all the angels of God worship Him," says the writer of the Epistle to the Hebrews, 1:6. Peter refers to Him as "our Lord and Saviour Jesus Christ," II Peter 3:18. In the book of Revelation we read, "Worthy is the Lamb that hath been slain to receive the power, and riches, and wisdom, and might, and honor, and glory, and blessing. . . . Unto Him that sitteth on the throne, and unto the Lamb, be the blessing, and the honor, and the glory, and the dominion, for ever and ever," 5:12,13.

At the beginning of each of Paul's letters we find a prayer in which he couples together on a plane of complete equality the names "God our Father" and "the Lord Jesus Christ" as the common source from which the gifts of grace and peace are sought. Yet to Paul there were not two objects of worship, nor two sources of blessing, but one. In I Cor. 8:4-6 he calls attention to the fact that we know that "there is no God but one." And the Apostolic Benediction—"The grace of the Lord Jesus Christ, and the love of God, and the communion of the Holy Spirit, be with you all," II Cor. 13:14, which is a prayer addressed to Christ for His grace, to the Father for His love, and to the Holy Spirit for His fellowship—is designed to exhibit at once the unity and the distinctness of the three Persons of the Trinity. On this formula, as in that of baptism, the Deity, and consequently the equality, of each of the Persons of the Godhead is taken for granted; and no other interpretation is rationally possible except that which the Church has held down through the ages, namely, that God exists in three Persons and that these three Persons are one in substance and equal in power and glory.

Consequently, when we compare these verses in which prayer and worship are ascribed to Christ with verses in which the unity of God and His exclusive right to the worship of men are set forth, such as, "Look unto me, and be ye saved, all the ends of the earth; for I am God, and there is none else," Is. 45:22; "We know that . . . there is no God but one," I Cor. 8:4; and, "Thus saith the Lord, Cursed is the man that trusteth in man, and that maketh flesh his arm," Jer. 17:5, together with the repeated condemnation of idolatry, we are faced with this dilemma: Either the Christian doctrine of the Deity of Christ is true, or the Scriptures are self-contradictory; either the Scriptures recognize more Gods than one, or Christ, together with the Father and the Holy Spirit, is that one God.

Thus throughout the New Testament Christ is everywhere set forth as the proper object of prayer and worship. The relation which He sustains to His people is that which God alone can sustain to rational creatures. As Dr. Warfield has well said, "To the writers of the New Testament the recognition of Jesus as Lord was the mark of a Christian; and all their religious emotions turned on Him. . . . To the heathen observers of the early Christians, their most distinguishing characteristic, which differentiated them from all others, was that they sang praises to Christ as God."[5] And Dr. Hodge says: "Christ is the God of the Apostles and early Christians, in the sense that He is the object of all their religious affections. They regarded Him as the person to whom they specially belonged; to whom they were responsible for their moral conduct; to whom they had to account for their sins; for the use of their time and talents; who was ever present with them, dwelling in them, controlling their inward, as well as their outward life; whose love was the animating principle of their being; in whom they rejoiced as their present joy and as their everlasting portion. This recognition of their relation to Christ as their God, is constant and pervading, so that the evidence of it cannot be gathered up and stated in a polemic and didactic form. But every reader of the New Testament to whom Christ is a mere creature, however exalted, must feel himself to be out of communion with the Apostles and apostolic Christians, who avowed themselves and were universally recognized by others as being the worshippers of Christ. They knew that they were to stand before His judgment seat; that every act, thought, and word of theirs, and of every man who shall ever live, was to lie open to His omniscient eye; and that on His decision the destiny of every human soul was to depend.

---
5. *Christology and Criticism*, p. 372.

The Attributes of Deity are Ascribed to Christ 57

... True religion in their view consists not in the love or reverence of God, merely as the infinite Spirit, the Creator and Preserver of all things, but in the knowledge and love of Christ."[6]

12. JUDGMENT OF ALL MEN: The idea of final judgment occupies a prominent place in the teaching of Jesus. But not only did He emphasize the thought of judgment. He taught that He Himself is to be the Judge, and that as such He will pass on the merits and demerits of all men, assigning to each individual his eternal destiny. "For neither doth the Father judge any man," said Jesus, "but He hath given all judgment unto the Son . . . for the hour cometh, in which all that are in the tombs shall hear His voice, and shall come forth; they that have done good, unto the resurrection of life; and they that have done evil, unto the resurrection of judgment," John 5:22-29. In the great eschatological discourse in the twenty-fifth chapter of Matthew He pictures Himself as the final Judge of all the nations and as the "King": "But when the Son of Man shall come in His glory, and all the angels with Him, then shall He sit on the throne of His glory: and before Him shall be gathered all the nations: and He shall separate them one from another, as the shepherd separateth the sheep from the goats; and He shall set the sheep on His right hand, but the goats on the left. Then shall the King say unto them on His right hand, Come, ye blessed of my Father, inherit the kingdom prepared for you from the foundation of the world. . . . Then shall He say also unto them on the left hand, Depart from me, ye cursed, into the eternal fire which is prepared for the Devil and his angels. . . . And these shall go away into eternal punishment: but the righteous into eternal life," vss. 31-46. Even in the early part of His ministry, as recorded in the Sermon on the Mount,

---
6. *Systematic Theology,* I, 498.

Jesus pictures Himself as the Lord and Judge who determines human destiny: "Not every one that sayeth unto me, Lord, Lord, shall enter into the kingdom of heaven; but he that doeth the will of my Father who is in heaven. Many will say unto me in that day, Lord, Lord, did we not prophesy in thy name, and by thy name cast out demons, and by thy name do many mighty works? And then will I profess unto them, I never knew you: depart from me, ye that work iniquity," Matt. 7:21-23. Peter testifies that "this is He who is ordained of God to be the Judge of the living and the dead," Acts 10:42. And Paul says, "We must all be made manifest before the judgment-seat of Christ; that each one may receive the things done in the body, according to what he hath done, whether it be good or bad," II Cor. 5:10. Furthermore, it is generally acknowledged that the New Testament not only expresses the beliefs of those who wrote it, but that it also directly and indirectly bears witness to the beliefs of the early Christian community as a whole; and there is scarcely any better witness to the profound impression that Jesus made on the early Christian community than this, that they accepted His claims and trusted in Him even when He claimed to be the Judge of the world.

Thus we find that throughout the whole range of His activity Jesus does not hesitate to lay His hands on the highest prerogatives of Deity. He claims for Himself, and others readily ascribe to Him, all of the essential attributes of Deity: holiness, eternity, life, immutability, omnipotence, omniscience, omnipresence, creation, authority to forgive sins, the power to save the souls of men, the right to receive prayer and worship, and the authority to pass final judgment on all men. He promises to be to men all that God can be, and to do for them all that God can do, and so to be God in a more

The Attributes of Deity are Ascribed to Christ 59

ultimate sense than He is man. To the Unitarians and Modernists who deny the Deity of Christ but who claim to accept Him as a moral teacher it should be perfectly evident that His authority as an ethical teacher stands or falls with His claims to possess the attributes of Deity and to be the object of worship. For if as a mere man He asked and received worhip from other men and so led them into idolatry, how can He be considered an authority in teaching men the way to please God? How can we eulogize Him as proclaimer of the Beatitudes and the Golden Rule and at the same time condemn Him for usurping the prerogatives which belong to God alone? It is utterly impossible to accept Christ as a great teacher and yet deny His Deity. We can feel nothing but indignation toward those so-called leaders in the Church who, while rendering lip service to Christ, reject His Deity and criticize irreverently the inspired records of His Person and work. The alternative is clear: Either Jesus is God, or He is not good. Either He is supernatural or sub-normal. Either He was the Messiah as He claimed to be, or He was the greatest imposter that ever walked this earth. Either He possessed and still possesses power to save men, or He has succeeded in perpetrating a fraud which through the ages has victimized innumerably more people than has any other false system.

It is superabundantly clear that a merely human Jesus such as is imagined by the Unitarians and Modernists—a mere man who mistakenly thought of Himself as the Messiah possessed of supernatural power, rising from the dead, and sitting as judge over all peoples and nations—could never have made the impression on his followers that the historical Jesus made, and could never have become the source of the stream of religious influence which we call Christianity. The assumption that a deluded fanatic or a deliberate imposter could have given the world what is incomparably the loftiest moral and spiritual system that it has ever received is simply ridiculous. "Who is the liar but he that denieth that Jesus is the Christ? This is the antichrist, even he that denieth the Father and the Son. Whoever denieth the Son, the same hath not the Father; he that confesseth the Son hath the Father also," I John 2:22,23. No one who is familiar with Scripture evidence and who knows the influence that Christianity has had throughout the world during the past twenty centuries can reasonably deny that Christ was what He claimed to be, truly Divine and truly the Saviour of the world.

IX.

JESUS' LIFE THE FULFILLMENT OF A DIVINE PLAN

AS WE study the portrait of Jesus as it is presented in the four Gospels there is impressed upon us the teaching that He came to earth on a specific mission, and that His whole life was lived and His work of redemption was accomplished in accordance with a divinely predetermined plan. At least from the outset of the public ministry that plan lay before His mind in clear outline. He had no time to lose, yet He was never in a hurry. He was never the victim but always the master of circumstance. Unswerved by the opposition of men, He went unflinchingly forward with the work that had been ordained for Him in the counsels of eternity. His whole life was governed by a divine "must" or "necessity." "I must preach the good tidings of the kingdom of God to the other cities also: for therefore was I sent," Luke 4:43, said He early in His ministry. Mark tells us that "He began to teach them, that the Son of Man must suffer many things, and be rejected by the elders, and the chief priests, and the scribes, and be killed, and after three days rise again," 8:31. And on the resurrection morning the angel reminded the women that during His public ministry Jesus had foretold these very things. In discussing His pre-existence we have already cited verses which teach that He "came" or "was sent" to perform a specific mission. Particularly were the events concerned with His going out of the world a matter of Divine necessity. His final journey to Jerusalem, His rejection by the chief priests and elders, Judas' betrayal, His arrest, sufferings, death by crucifixion, and His resurrection on the third day, were not merely predicted but were presented as necessary in the fulfillment of His mission. And after His resurrection He said to the disciples: "These are my words which I spake unto you, while I was yet with you, that all things must needs be fulfilled, which are written in the law of Moses, and the prophets, and the psalms, concerning me. Then opened He their minds, that they might understand the Scriptures; and he said unto them, Thus it is written, that the Christ should suffer, and rise again from the dead the third day; and that repentance and remission of sins should be preached in His name unto all the nations, beginning from Jerusalem," Luke 24:44-47.

For a Divine Person to undertake such a mission involved humiliation at every point. Not only was there humiliation in the poverty, weariness and hunger which He endured, in the persistent opposition which was carried on by His opponents, in the public rejection of Him by the rulers in Church and State, and in His final suffering, death and burial. In the first placed it involved deep humiliation for a Divine Person to submit Himself to human birth, to exist as a helpless babe, and to experience for a period of thirty-three years the whole series of limitations and weaknesses to which human nature is subject. Yet His mission is represented as being in every step and stage of it voluntary and as having been carried through to complete fulfillment. Every suggestion of escape from it, whether by the use of His supernatural powers for personal gratification, or of evading or lessening His suffering, was treated by Him as a temptation from the Devil. He came into the world with the express purpose of making an atonement for sin through His own suffering and death; and the events which led up to that climax were determined in their precise order and time not for Him but by Him.

Jesus' Life the Fulfillment of a Divine Plan 63

"Determining all things, determined by none," says Dr. Warfield, "the life He actually lived, leading up to the death He actually died, is in the view of the Evangelists precisely the life which from the beginning He intended to live, ending in precisely the death in which, from the beginning, He intended this life to issue, undeflected by so much as a hair's breadth from the straight path He had from the start marked out for Himself in the fullest prevision and provision of all the so-called chances and changes which might befall Him. Not only were there no surprises in life for Jesus and no compulsions; there were not even 'influences,' as we speak of 'influences' in a merely human career. The mark of this life, as the Evangelists depict it, is its calm and quiet superiority to all circumstances and conditions, and to all the varied forces which sway other lives; its prime characteristics were voluntariness and independence. Neither His mother, nor His brethren, nor His disciples, nor the people He came to serve, nor His enemies bent on His destruction, nor Satan himself with his temptations, could move Him one step from His chosen path. When men seemed to prevail over Him they were but working His will; the great 'No one taketh my life away from me! I have power is lay it down, and I have power to take it again' (John 10:18), is but the enunciation for the supreme act, of the principle that governs all His movements. His own chosen pathway ever lay fully displayed before His feet; on it His feet fell quietly, and they found the way always unblocked. What He did, He came to do; and He carried out His programme with unwavering purpose and indefectible certitude."[1]

Certainly the Gospel writers present the suffering and death of Christ not as an accident or calamity, but as an achieve-

---
1. *Biblical Doctrines*, p. 74.

ment, an accomplishment. At the time of the Transfiguration Moses and Elijah appeared to Jesus and "spake of His decease which He was about to accomplish at Jerusalem," Luke 9:31. "I have a baptism to be baptized with; and how am I straitened till it be accomplished," Luke 12:50, said He with reference to the ordeal which lay ahead. When the time came for Him to suffer God measured to Him the contents of the cup, and determined what He should endure. He, not His enemies, set the date of His death. Strange and incredible though His crucifixion and death seemed to the disciples, it was all according to plan, designed to become the ground of forgiveness for men, the doorway into a new and abiding kingdom of righteousness and life.

In the book of Acts this same emphasis on the sovereignty and over-ruling providence of God as it relates to the events of Jesus' life is set forth clearly and strongly. The crucifixion, which is beyond doubt the most sinful event in the history of the world, is even declared to have been foreordained. "For of a truth in this city against thy holy servant Jesus, who thou didst anoint, both Herod and Pontius Pilate, with the Gentiles and the people of Israel, were gathered together, to do whatsoever thy hand and thy counsel foreordained to come to pass," Acts 4:27,28. And further: "Him being delivered up by the determinate counsel and foreknowledge of God, ye by the hands of lawless men did crucify and slay," Acts 2:23; "The things which God foreshadowed by the mouth of all the prophets, that His Christ should suffer, He thus fulfilled," Acts 3:18; "For they that dwelt in Jerusalem, and their rulers, because they knew Him not, nor the voice of the prophets which are read every Sabbath, fulfilled them in condemning Him. And though they found no cause of death in Him, yet asked they of Pilate that He should be

Jesus' Life the Fulfillment of a Divine Plan 65

slain. And when they had fulfilled all things that were written of Him, they took Him down from the tree, and laid Him in a tomb," Acts 13:27-29.

But while these things were foreordained and predicted, they were carried out by agents who acted by their own free choice and who were therefore fully responsible for what they did. Those who abused Jesus were ignorant of the fact that they were laying on Him precisely the burden of suffering that God had ordained that His Christ should bear. Hence through all this we see the sovereignty of God marvelously displayed in that the actions of Christ's enemies, sinful though they were because done with evil motives, were overruled for the redemption of the world.

There is, of course, no basis whatsoever for the Modernistic view that Jesus first aimed at a temporal kingdom only to abandon the idea when the people failed to respond. The facts are that, first, He repudiated temporal power in the temptations immediately after His baptism; and, secondly, in His earliest preaching, particularly in the Sermon on the Mount, the requirements for membership in His kingdom were spiritual, faith and repentance.

Furthermore, in this connection it is important to notice the air of authority with which Jesus spoke. There had been many prophets in Israel who prefaced their words with "Thus saith the Lord," and then proceeded to speak God's word to the people sternly and uncompromisingly. But Jesus went much farther. He did not refer to an authority outside of Himself but, placing Himself in the relation of God to His people, spoke in His own name and as the final authority. In the Sermon on the Mount He spoke as the sovereign Law-Giver, and proceeded to elaborate more fully or to modify the word of God as given in the Old Testament. Repeatedly

His commands are equated with the law of God: "Ye have heard that it was said . . . . But I say unto you . . . ." Those who are persecuted for His sake are equated with the prophets who suffered for the cause of God, Matt. 5:11,12. He assume the role of the final Judge in admitting people into, or in excluding them from, the kingdom of heaven: "Not every one that saith unto me, Lord, Lord shall enter the kingdom of heaven; but he that doeth the will of my Father who is in heaven. Many will say unto me in that day, Lord, Lord, did we not prophesy in thy name, and by thy name cast out demons, and by thy name do many mighty works? And then will I profess unto them, I never knew you: depart from me, ye that work iniquity," Matt. 7:21-23. We are told that at the conclusion of the Sermon on the Mount "the multitudes were astonished at His teaching: for He taught them as one having authority, and not as their scribes," Matt. 7:28,29. He assumed authority over the sacred ordinances of Israel, not only over the law but also over the temple and the Sabbath. "One greater than the temple is here. . . . The Son of Man is Lord of the Sabbath," Matt. 12:6,8. To the disciples He said, "Heaven and earth shall pass away, but my words shall not pass away," Matt. 24:35. The men of Nineveh and the queen of the south are to rise up in the judgment and condemn that generation because He, the greater than Jonah who preached to the Ninevites and than Solomon whose glories attracted the queen of Sheba, was present among them and had given them greater opportunities than had been given to any former generation. He asserts that He and the Father are one (John 10:30), and that the Father is in Him, and He in the Father (John 10:38). To believe on Him is to believe on God (John 12:44); to see Him is to see the Father (John 14:9); and all are to honor the Son, even as they honor the Father (John

Jesus' Life the Fulfillment of a Divine Plan 67

5:23). For us who are accustomed to think of the law, the temple and the Sabbath in the light of New Testament teaching and to look to Jesus as our divine Master, it is hard to realize how revolutionary all of this must have sounded to the orthodox Jew.

While we are told that "the Son of Man came not to be ministered unto, but to minister, and to give His life a ransom for many," Matt. 20:28, we are to note that His manner of behaviour throughout the period of his early life was distinctly not that of a servant. He claimed and received obedience and reverence, and His followers recognized Him as their Master and Lord. We have already seen that He applied to Himself and accepted from others the highest titles. Even in this saying the title "Son of Man" and the assertion that He "came" on a particular mission sets Him apart as a transcendent Being. It was not the *manner* of His earthly life, but the mere *fact* that He, the Heavenly One, had become incarnate and subjected Himself to the limitations of earth that needed explanation. And in this verse He gives that explanation, which was that He might render a particular service to His people in redeeming them from the power of sin.

There can be no doubt but that in His teaching Jesus presented Himself not as one needing salvation but as the Saviour of men, not as a member of the Church but as the head of the Church, not as the example but as the object of faith, not merely as a supplicant praying to God but as the one to whom prayer is to be made, not merely as a teacher of men but as their sovereign Lord. If Jesus was only a man, not essentially different from the rest of us, then, of course, there would be no reason why we should accept His statements as binding on our conscience. In that case we would be warranted in classing Him along with Socrates, Plato, Confucius, etc., as one of the world's wisest and most influential teachers. But if He was the Person He claimed to be, Deity incarnate, He has the fullest right to speak to us in this authoritative tone and we do but show ordinary common sense when we heed His voice as the voice of God.

X.

THE MIRACLES OF JESUS

ANOTHER special proof of the Deity of Christ is that afforded by His miracles. A miracle may be defined as an event in the external world, wrought by the immediate power of God, and designed to accredit a message or a messenger. It is, in short, an appearance of the supernatural within the realm of the natural. The miracles wrought by Jesus differed from those wrought by the prophets or the apostles in that they were wrought by His own inherent power rather than by power delegated to Him. When the prophets or the apostles wrought miracles they expressly disclaimed that it was by any power within themselves. When the waters of the Red Sea were divided Moses ascribed the work to God (Ex. 14:13), as also did Joshua (Joshua 3:5), Elijah (I Kings 18:36), and the other prophets when similar marvelous works were performed; and in the New Testament when Peter and John had healed the lame man at the door of the temple Peter very quickly met the curiosity of the crowd with these words: "Why marvel ye at this man? or why fasten ye your eyes on us, as though by our own power or godliness we had made him to walk?" Acts 3:12, and when at Lystra Paul healed a lame man and the multitudes were ready to offer sacrifice to him and Barnabas they sprang forward and confessed themselves to be "men of like passions" with them and gave God the glory (Acts 14:15). But when Jesus healed the sick, or cast out demons, or raised the dead, or calmed the raging sea, it was by the exercise of His own limitless power. "The works that

I do in my Father's name, these bear witness of me," said He to the Jews in Jerusalem, John 10:25. "If I do not the works of my Father, believe me not. But if I do them, though ye believe not me, believe the works; that ye may know and understand that the Father is in me, and I in the Father," John 10:37, 38. "If I had not done among them the works which none other did, they had not had sin: but now have they both seen and hated both me and my Father," John 15:24. When the disciples of John the Baptist came to ask if He were the Messiah He did not give them a yes or no answer but, letting the evidence speak for itself, said: "Go tell John the things which ye hear and see: the blind receive their sight, and the lame walk, the lepers are cleansed, and the deaf hear, and the dead are raised up, and the poor have good tidings preached to them," Matt. 11:4, 5. Since the laws of nature have been ordained of God they can be changed or suspended only by Him. And in every instance where Jesus exercised that power He manifested His glory and thus gave visible proof of His Deity to those who had eyes to see.

The number of miracles worked by Jesus was undoubtedly large; for while only about thirty-five or forty are recorded —these being given as examples which showed His power in healing diseases which were incurable so far as human help was concerned, in raising the dead, in demonstrating His power over the forces of nature, etc.,—there are occasional blanket statements to the effect that "Jesus went about in all Galilee, teaching in their synagogues, and preaching the Gospel of the kingdom, and healing all manner of disease, and all manner of sickness among the people," Matt. 4:23; "And when the sun was setting, all they that had any sick with divers diseases brought them unto Him; and He laid His hands on every one of them, and healed them," Luke 4:40. See also

Matt. 4:24; 15:30; etc. Hence for a time disease and death were reduced to a minimum throughout the land,—a blessing which in itself, because of the almost complete lack of medicines and surgical skill in that day, must have meant a radical change in the life of the nation.

But more important, of course, than the miracles wrought by Jesus was His teaching, which in its insight and its foresight was as supernatural as were His miracles and manifested His Deity as clearly as did they. Moreover, it was with authority, very much unlike that of the scribes and Pharisees. The net result of both His teaching and His miracles was that His fame spread through all parts of the country, even to such an extent that He could not openly enter into the cities because of the multitudes which thronged about Him. And that, in turn, rendered all the more heinous and inexcusable the opposition of the scribes and Pharisees.

That the miracles of Jesus were designed to prove His Deity and to inspire faith on the part of the people, and that they did have exactly that effect on unprejudiced minds, is clearly stated in the Gospel records. "This beginning of signs did Jesus in Cana of Galilee, and manifested His glory; and His disciples believed on Him," John 2:11. Mark records that "the common people heard Him gladly," 12:37. Luke says that after healing a leper early in His ministry "great multitudes came together to hear," 5:15, and Mark adds that "they came to Him from every quarter," 1:45. The man whose eyes were opened after he washed in the pool of Siloam rebuked the unbelief of the Pharisees with these words: "Why, herein is the marvel, that ye know not whence He is, and yet He opened mine eyes. . . . Since the world began it was never heard that any one opened the eyes of a man born blind. If this man were not from God, He could do nothing," John

9:30-33. When Lazarus was raised from the dead "many of the Jews, who came to Mary and beheld that which He did, believed on Him," John 11:45. Thomas, the most skeptical of all of the disciples, when confronted with the resurrection body of Jesus, was fully convinced and cried out, "My Lord and my God," John 20:28. Certainly nothing less than this conclusion, as also the conclusion to which Peter came, "Thou art the Christ, the Son of the living God," Matt. 16:16, can explain the miracles of the New Testament. Jesus Himself marvelled that any people could see these mighty works which so wonderfully displayed the limitless power and wisdom and love of God and still not believe (Mark 6:1-6), and in burning language He foretold the judgments which were to be visited on the cities that rejected these signs (Matt. 10:1-15; Luke 10:1-15).

The miracles of Jesus are, of course, an integral part of the New Testament record. They cannot be rejected without destroying the credibility of the entire record. The problem raised is not merely that of the bare possibility of supernatural works, but that of the supernatural Person of Jesus and His redemptive work, plus miracles. We very readily admit that if we were to hear of even one such event having been performed by a mere man anywhere in the world today we would not believe it. The absolutely wrong way to study the miracles is to look at them as detached and isolated happenings having no connection with any plan of redemption. If Christ was what He declared Himself to be, Deity incarnate, living a perfectly normal yet sinless life in this world and giving Himself up to suffer and die in man's stead and for his sin, then the working of miracles as a means of accrediting His Person and message would appear to have been a most natural and normal accompaniment for such a life. In fact, we can hardly conceive of God working out such a plan of redemption without just such displays of supernatural power as are recorded in the Gospels. The miracles are, as it were, sparks emitted by the fires within. Nowhere was this more convincingly displayed than in the Transfiguration, at which time the limitations of earth were partially removed and the glory of the Divine Christ shone out through the veil of flesh. We can no more separate the miraculous and the non-miraculous elements in the Bible than we can separate the body and soul in man. A Bible without a supernatural Christ and supernatural works would be like a temple without God. Hence, the question, Did the miracles really happen? is subordinate to the questions, Who was Jesus? and, What was the nature of His work? If we get those questions settled correctly we shall have no difficulty in believing the miracles.

XI.

IMPORTANCE OF BELIEF IN THE DEITY OF CHRIST

THE Deity of Christ is thus taught in Scripture so explicitly and repeatedly that the question is settled for all those who accept the Bible as the word of God. There can be no question but that Jesus Himself as He is portrayed in the New Testament records presented Himself as God incarnate. Nor is there any doubt but that the writers of the New Testament personally held this same high estimate of Him and worshipped Him as God, or that the Church in all ages in all its great branches, whether Roman Catholic, Greek Catholic, Lutheran, Reformed, Presbyterian, Episcopal, Methodist, Baptist, or Congregational, as its faith has been expressed through its creeds and hymns and devotional writings, has likewise conceived of Him. And throughout the ages the great mass of those who have read the New Testament have come to the same conclusion.

In view of this great mass of evidence we are completely unable to understand how any fair-minded person can rise up and say, as do the Unitarians and Modernists, that Christ was not Deity, or that He did not claim Deity. In fact, we must go farther and say that such opposition appears to be based on nothing other than blind opposition and a determination not to accept that evidence no matter how clear and strong it may be. Any denial of the Deity of Christ, together with the implication that He was merely a great teacher or

Importance of Belief in the Deity of Christ 75

prophet, gives one a viewpoint other than that from which the Scriptures are written and makes it impossible for him to comprehend the system of truth that is revealed in Scripture. Such denial throws one out of harmony with the great Source of wisdom and truth, which is God, and causes him to attempt to explain intellectually that which can only be discerned spiritually.

The pre-eminent importance of the doctrine of the Deity of Christ in the Christian system is shown by the fact that this is the test by which we are to distinguish between true and false prophets, between spirits which are of God and spirits which are not of God. The Apostle John, after giving the warning, "Beloved, believe not every spirit, but prove the spirits, whether they are of God; because many false prophets are gone out into the world," adds these words: "Hereby know ye the Spirit of God: every spirit that confesseth that Jesus Christ is come in the flesh is of God: every spirit that confesseth not Jesus is not of God: and this is the spirit of the antichrist, whereof we have heard that it cometh, and now it is in the world already," I John 4:1-3. Here we are plainly told that every one who acknowledges that Christ has come in the flesh is of God, and that every one who denies the Deity of Christ is antichrist. Regardless of how eloquent the speaker may be, how pleasing or magnetic his personality, how widespread his influence, or even how sincere his motives, the prophet or preacher or teacher who denies the Deity of Christ is branded in Scripture as a false prophet or preacher or teacher. And to the same effect Paul says: "No man speaking in the Spirit of God saith, Jesus is anathema; and no man can say, Jesus is Lord, but in the Holy Spirit," I Cor. 12:3. Here Paul declares that only by the spiritual insight which the Holy Spirit gives as He regenerates a soul can that soul form a true judgment of the Deity of Christ. No one recognizes Christ as Lord and as his Lord unless he has been born again. The man who looks at Jesus only with his own unenlightened eyes sees in Him only a man, perhaps a great man with many lofty principles and ideals, yet a man who has claimed too much for Himself and who has committed blasphemy by calling himself the Son of God. But when the Holy Spirit comes into his life, renewing and enlightening him spiritually, he then sees himself a guilty, condemned sinner who merits nothing but God's wrath and punishment. But he is also given to see, by the eye of faith, that Jesus is the Son of God, that He lived on this earth, that He was crucified for the sins of His people, that He arose from the grave, and that He now reigns from heaven. Never does a mortal man see the Lord Jesus thus, and never does he accept Him as his Lord, unless it is so given him by the Holy Spirit. Thus Paul says that no person can acknowledge Jesus as Lord unless he has been enlightened by the Holy Spirit. And, incidentally, in these words he also tells us that the person who does thus acknowledge Jesus as Lord has been regenerated and is therefore assured of salvation.

In concluding our discussion of this great basic doctrine of the Deity of Christ we can do no better than to quote the words of Dr. Charles Hodge. Says he: "Whoever believes that Jesus is the Son of God, i.e., whoever believes that Jesus of Nazareth is God manifested in the flesh, and loves and obeys Him as such, is declared to be born of God. Any one who denies that truth, is declared to be antichrist, denying both the Father and the Son, for the denial of the one is the denial of the other. The same truth is expressed by another Apostle, who says, 'If our gospel is hid it is hid to them that

Importance of Belief in the Deity of Christ 77

are lost, in whom the god of this world hath blinded the minds of them which believe not, lest they should see the glory of God as it shines in the face of Jesus Christ.' They are lost, according to this Apostle, who do not see, as well as believe, Jesus to be God dwelling in the flesh. Hence such effects are ascribed to the knowledge of Christ, and to faith in Him; such hopes are entertained of the glory and blessedness of being with Him, as would be impossible or irrational if Christ were not the true God. He is our life. He that hath the Son hath life. He that believes on Him shall live forever. It is not we that live, but Christ that liveth in us. Our life is hid with Christ in God. We are complete in Him, wanting nothing. Though we have not seen Him, yet believing in Him, we rejoice in Him with joy unspeakable. It is because Christ is God, because He is possessed of all divine perfections, and because He loved us and gave Himself for us, and hath redeemed us and made us kings and priests unto God that the Spirit of God says, 'If any man love not the Lord Jesus Christ, let him be anathema.' The denial of the divinity of the Son of God, the refusal to receive, love, trust, worship, and serve Him as such, is the ground of the hopeless condemnation of all who hear and reject the Gospel. And to the justice of this condemnation all rational creatures, holy and unholy, justified and condemned, will say, Amen. The divinity of Christ is too plain a fact, and too momentous a truth, to be innocently rejected. Those are saved who truly believe it, and those are already lost who have not eyes to see it. He that believeth not is condemned already, because he hath not believed on the name of the only begotten Son of God. He that believeth on the Son hath everlasting life; and he that believeth not the Son shall not see life, but the wrath of God abideth on him. It is the doctrine of the New Testament, therefore, that the spiritual apprehension and the sincere recognition of the Godhead of the Redeemer constitutes the life of the soul. It is in its own nature eternal life; and the absence or want of this faith and knowledge is spiritual and eternal death. Christ is our life; and therefore he that hath not the Son hath not life."[1]

---

1. *Systematic Theology*, I, 498.

XII.

THE HUMANITY OF CHRIST

IN ANSWER to the question, "Who is the Redeemer of God's elect?" the Shorter Catechism says: "The only Redeemer of God's elect is the Lord Jesus Christ, who, being the eternal Son of God, became man, and so was, and continueth to be God, and man, in two distinct natures, and one person, for ever." And in answer to the question, "How did Christ, being the Son of God, become man? the Catechism says: "Christ, the Son of God, became man, by taking to Himself a true body and a reasonable (i.e., reasoning) soul, being conceived by the power of the Holy Ghost, in the womb of the Virgin Mary, and born of her, yet without sin."

While as we have seen in the preceding chapter Christ was Deity in the highest sense, possessed of all the attributes and titles of God and free from any taint of sin or error, we are not to forget that He was also perfect humanity, bone of our bone and flesh of our flesh, and that during His earthly career He lived on this earth as a man among men, subject to all of the trials and temptations and sufferings which are common to men. He is as truly one with us on the side of His humanity as He is one with God on the side of His Deity. As a babe He came to consciousness; as a child and youth He "advanced in wisdom and stature, and in favor with God and men"; and as a man He fulfilled perfectly the divine ideal of what God made man and meant man to be. All of the rest of us are only sketches or suggestions of manhood, having had our speech and action and sometimes even our bodies grotesquely marred by the destructive influences of sin. He alone had a strictly normal development, having been born into the world without the fatal entail of original sin, and having grown from childhood to manhood governed always by purity and righteousness. From the mouth of His mother He first learned the sacred things of God, and at her knee He often knelt to pray. He grew up in the obscure town of Nazareth. Doubtless the wonders of His infancy were kept a secret by Joseph and Mary, although after His crucifixion Mary may have related these to the intimate group of the disciples and thus they may have found their way into Matthew's and Luke's Gospel. In all probability as He grew up His companions and the family saw nothing in Him to lead them to believe that He was a supernatural Being, but were only impressed with His remarkable mental force and moral purity. It seems probable that Joseph died before Jesus entered upon His public ministry, and that since He was the firstborn the responsibility of supporting His mother and the rest of the family fell upon His shoulders. As a carpenter He knew what every-day toil was. How much we should have missed if the Last Adam had appeared on earth as did the first Adam, mature! Instead He has passed through all the stages of human experience, from childhood to manhood. He knows human life fully, by personal experience.

The reality of Jesus' human nature and the genuineness of His human life is everywhere assumed and endlessly illustrated throughout the Scriptures. The first promise of a Redeemer, recorded in Genesis 3:15, to the effect that the seed of the woman should bruise the head of the serpent, indicated quite clearly that God purposed to use a human agent. The promise was made to Abraham that the everlasting covenant would be established with his seed (Gen. 17:19; 22:18),

The Humanity of Christ

which promise Paul says was fulfilled not in the Jewish people as such but in Christ (Gal. 3:16, 29). David was promised that His seed should sit upon His throne for ever (II Sam. 7:12-16; II Chr. 6:16). "Of the fruit of thy body will I set upon thy throne," Ps. 132:11. Isaiah foretold the advent of the Messiah (9:6, 7), even saying that He should be born of a virgin (7:14). And Micah said that He should be born in Bethlehem (5:2).

In dozens of places the New Testament ascribes to Jesus the reactions and experiences which are common to human nature. The following will serve as a fairly representative list. (1) birth: "Now when Jesus was born in Bethlehem," Matt. 2:1; "There is born to you this day in the city of David a Saviour," Luke 2:11. (2) Growth: "And the child grew, and waxed strong, filled with wisdom," Luke 2:40; "And Jesus advanced in wisdom and stature, and in favor with God and men," Luke 2:52. (3) Fatigue: "Jesus therefore, being wearied with His journey, sat thus by the well," John 4:6. (4) Sleep: "The boat was covered with the waves: but He was asleep," Matt. 8:24; "And they awoke Him," Mark 4:38. (5) Hunger: "And when He had fasted forty days and forty nights, He afterward hungered," Matt. 4:2; "Now in the morning as He returned to the city, He hungered," Matt. 21:18. (6) Thirst: "Jesus . . . saith, I thirst," John 19:28. (7) Indignation: "But when Jesus saw it, He was moved with indignation," Mark 10:14; "And when He had looked round about on them with anger, being grieved at the hardening of their heart," Mark 3:5. (8) Compassion: "But when He saw the multitudes, He was moved with compassion for them," Matt. 9:36; "And being moved with compassion (toward the leper), He stretched forth His hand, and touched him," Mark 1:41. (9) Love:

"Jesus looking upon him loved him," Mark 10:21; "One of His disciples, whom Jesus loved," John 13:23. (10) Joy: "These things have I spoken unto you, that my joy may be in you, and that your joy may be made full," John 15:11. (11) Sorrow and anxiety: "And He . . . began to be sorrowful and sore troubled," Matt. 26:37; "Jesus wept," John 11:35; "Now is my soul troubled," John 12:27. (12) Temptation: "Then was Jesus led up of the Spirit into the wilderness to be tempted of the Devil," Matt 4:1; "For we have not a high priest that cannot be touched with the feeling of our infirmities; but one that hath been in all points tempted like as we are, yet without sin," Heb. 4:15; "For in that He Himself hath suffered being tempted, He is able to succor them that are tempted," Heb. 2:18. (13) Prayer: "He went up into the mountain apart to pray," Matt. 14:23; "Who in the days of His flesh, having offered up prayers and supplications with strong crying and tears," Heb. 5:7; "And being in an agony He prayed more earnestly; and His sweat became as it were great drops of blood falling down upon the ground," Luke 22:44. (14) Suffering: "He was wounded for our transgressions, He was bruised for our iniquities; the chastisement of our peace was upon Him; and with His stripes we are healed," Is. 53:5; "Thus it is written, that the Christ should suffer," Luke 24:46; "Though He was a Son, yet learned obedience by the things which He suffered," Heb. 5:8; "for it became Him . . . to make the Author of their salvation perfect through suffering," Heb. 2:10. (15) Death: "And Jesus cried with a loud voice, and yielded up His spirit," Matt. 27:50; "Christ died for our sins according to the Scriptures," I Cor. 15:3.

Thus we are given to understand that Jesus was a truly human person, that He exercised the normal powers and was

The Humanity of Christ

subject to the normal reactions of human nature. The completeness of our Lord's human nature is made plain by the writer of the Epistle to the Hebrews when he says that "in all things" He was "made like unto His brethren" (2:17). He expressly called Himself "man": "Ye seek to kill me, a man that hath told you the truth," John 8:40; and He is called "man" by others: "Pilate saith unto them, Behold, the man!" John 19:5; "Jesus of Nazareth, a man approved of God unto you," Acts 2:22; "One Mediator also between God and men, Himself man, Jesus Christ," I Tim. 2:5. The genealogies given in Matt. 1:1-17 and Luke 3:23-28 make plain His human descent, and prove Him to have been the royal and legal heir of David. And the title, "Son of Man," regardless of how much more it may mean, certainly means that He was truly human. Down through the ages the Christian Church has always believed that her Christ was not only Divine but also human.

The limitations of Jesus in the realm of knowledge present an interesting study. We have already noted that He "advanced in wisdom," as well as in stature and in favor with God and men. But as man He did not and never can become omniscient, for the simple reason that human souls by their very nature are finite. He "marvelled" at the faith of the centurion, Luke 7:9. In one of the discourses given during His last week on earth He specifically told the disciples that He did not know the time of the end of the world: "But of that day and hour knoweth no one, not even the angels of heaven, neither the Son, but the Father only," Matt. 24:36 (see also Mark 13:32). In other Scripture we are given to understand that in the plan of God it is not intended that men should know when the end of the world is coming. Hence there was no need or occasion for that revelation to be made to men. And since Jesus Himself was true man His own human soul was subject to the same limitation. The Holy Spirit revealed to the human soul of Jesus many things concerning the future; but this was not among them. As Dr. J. Ritchie Smith has observed, however, "It was only the time of His coming that was hidden from Him. The precedents, concommitants, and consequences He foresaw and foretold. This single acknowledgement of ignorance serves to confirm our faith in Him by assuring us that He taught only what He knew. His ignorance pertained to His human nature, and He recognized the limits of His knowledge because they were self-imposed. He is the only man that ever lived who could describe the boundaries of His knowledge with absolute precision. There was with Him no region of speculation or conjecture intermediate between certain knowledge and conscious ignorance, as in the case of all men besides. He did not suppose or infer. He knew or He did not know, and the line of division was to Him precise and clear. Whenever He speaks, therefore, He speaks with authority."[1]

In a number of other instances Jesus asked and received information from human sources, but used supernatural power as He dealt further with the situations. Although when touched by the woman with the issue of blood He asked, "Who touched my garments?" He immediately manifested His power to heal her of the affliction (Mark 5:25-34). While the news of Lazarus' sickness was brought to him by human messengers, He knew without any further message that Lazarus was dead, and that this death was not to be permanent but that it was "for the glory of God, that the Son of God may be glorified thereby." He asked, "Where have ye laid him?" and wept with the bereaved sisters; yet He put forth super-

---

1. *Studies in the Gospel of John*, p. 136.

The Humanity of Christ 85

natural power and raised him from the dead, John 11:1-44. In Mark 11:12,13 we read: "And on the morrow, when they were come from Bethany, He hungered. And seeing a fig tree afar off having leaves, He came, if haply He might find anything thereon: and when He came to it, He found nothing but leaves"; yet at the same time He had power to wither it away from the roots (vss. 14, 20).

Concerning this general subject Dr. Warfield says: "Jesus Himself has told us that He was ignorant of the time of the day of judgment (Mark 13:32); He repeatedly is represented as seeking through questions, which undoubtedly were not asked only to give the appearance of a dependence upon information from without that was not real with Him: He is made to express surprise; and to make trial of new circumstances; and the like. There are no human traits lacking to the picture that is drawn of Him: He was open to temptation; He was conscious of dependence on God; He was a man of prayer; He knew a 'will' within Him that might conceivably be opposed to the will of God; He exercised faith; He learned obedience by the things that He suffered. It was not merely the mind of a man that was in Him, but the heart of a man—a man without error and sin—is, and must be conceived to have grown, as it is proper for a man to grow, not only during His youth, but continually through life, not alone in knowledge, but in wisdom, and not alone in wisdom, but 'in reverence and charity'—in moral strength and in beauty of holiness alike." He then goes on to state that Jesus continued to increase in wisdom and in all of the traits of His humanity, not only during His entire earthly life but that He continues to do so even since the time of His ascension: "For Christ, just because He is the *risen* Christ, is man and true man—all that man is, with all that is involved in being man

—through all the ages and unto the eternity of the eternities.

"We may not fear, therefore, that we may emphasize too strongly the true, the complete humanity of Christ. All that man as man is, that Christ is to eternity. The Reformed Theology which it is our happiness to inherit, has never hesitated to face the fact and rejoice in it, with all its implications. With regard to knowledge, for example, it has not shrunk from recognizing that Christ, as man, had a finite knowledge and must continue to have a finite knowledge for ever. Human nature is ever finite, it declares, and is no more capable of infinite *charismata* than of the infinite *idiomata* or attributes of the divine nature; so that it is certain that the knowledge of Christ's human nature is not and can never be the infinite wisdom of God itself. . . . It is again nothing but gain, to realize in all its fulness that our Lord was man even as we are men, made 'in all things like unto His brethren' (Heb. 2:17) . . .

"Alongside of these clear declarations and rich indications of His true and complete humanity, there runs an equally pervasive attribution to Him of all that belongs to Deity. If, for example, He is represented as not knowing this or that matter of fact (Mark 13:32), He is equally represented as knowing all things (John 21:17; John 16:30). If He is represented as acquiring information from without, asking questions and expressing surprise, He is equally represented as knowing without human information all that occurs or has occurred—the secret prayer of Nathanael (John 1:47), the whole life of the Samaritan woman (John 4:29), the very thoughts of His enemies (Matt. 9:4), all that is in man (John 2:25). Nor are these two classes of facts kept separate; they are rather interlaced in the most amazing manner. If it is by human informants that He is told of Lazarus' sick-

The Humanity of Christ

ness (John 11:3,6), it is of no human information that He knows him to be dead (John 11:11,14); if He asks 'Where have ye laid him?' and weeps with the sorrowing sister, He knows from the beginning (John 11:11) what His might should acomplish for the assuagement of this grief. Everywhere, in a word, we see a double life revealed before us in the dramatization of the actions of Jesus among men; not, indeed, in the sense that He is represented as acting inconsistently, or is inconsistently represented as acting now in one order and now in another; but rather in the sense that a duplex life is attributed to Him as His constant possession. If all that man is is attributed to Him, no less is all that God is attributed to Him, and the one attribution is no more pervasive than the other."[2]

Something of the importance of a correct doctrine of the humanity of Christ can be seen when we look at the errors into which the Roman Catholics have been led. They have emphasized His majesty and Deity to the almost total exclusion of His human qualities, with the result that they have come to think of both the Father and the Son as far removed from them. Almost invariably their pictures and images have represented the human Christ either as a helpless babe in a manger, or a dead Christ on a cross. Yet through all this they have continued to feel the need of a Divine-Human Mediator, One who as man can act as their true representative when He stands before the throne of God, and One who as Deity is able to intercede effectively with God. But since the Roman Catholic theology did not present this kind of a Mediator they have been forced to invent something else, and in their groping they have turned to the idolatrous worship of the Virgin Mary. They have hailed her as the

---
2. Article in *The Bible Student*, Jan., 1900.

"Mother of God" and have enthroned her as the "Queen of Heaven," thus for all practical purposes exalting her to a position of equality with God. We say this, not because we wish to give Mary any less honor than that which is her just due as the most blessed of women, but because we consider the Roman Catholic practice very misleading and wholly without Scripture warrant. Those who know the Jesus who is set forth in the New Testament find Him to be not only a man but the most sympathetic and the most approachable of men. Witness the readiness of the mothers to bring their children to Him, the ease with which the woman of Samaria entered into conversation with Him at the well, His deep sympathy for Mary and Martha at the death of their brother Lazarus. The poor, rough, uncultured fishermen of Galilee became His intimate and trusted friends. And we who live nearly two thousand years after these events find ourselves bound to Him with strong personal ties of love and friendship. To us, as to the early Christians, He says, "Ye are my friends." Although He is our Creator and Lord, if we trust and obey Him it is not presumptuous for us to call Him our Friend; and in fact we have not fully entered upon our inheritance in Him unless we do know Him not only as our Creator and Lord but also as our Friend. To the disciples He said, "No longer do I call you servants; for the servant knoweth not what his lord doeth: but I have called you friends; for all things that I have heard from my Father I have made known unto you," John 15:15. And from age to age He stands saying, "Come unto me, all ye that labor and are heavy laden, and I will give you rest," Matt. 11:28. Every true Christian, conscious of what Jesus has done for him, should feel that in a true sense he, like the disciple John, can designate himself as "the disciple whom Jesus loved." What a serious error it is, then, for any one to suppose that this our most intimate and loving Friend can be approached only through the intercession of some one else. Such practice pushes the Saviour far away and robs the Christian of one of his most precious possessions.

XIII.

THE HUMILIATION OF CHRIST

THE Apostle Paul tells us that Christ in order that He might accomplish His work of redemption "humbled" Himself (Phil. 2:8). The meaning of this is perhaps expressed more clearly and briefly in the Shorter Catechism than anywhere else when in answer to the question, "Wherein did Christ's humiliation consist?" the answer is given: "Christ's humiliation consisted in His being born, and that in low condition, made under the law, undergoing the miseries of this life, the wrath of God, and the cursed death of the cross; in being buried, and continuing under the power of death for a time."

According to this statement the first stage in the humiliation of Christ was His birth. For the Prince of Glory, who partakes of the same nature as the Father, to have condescended to take into personal and permanent union with Himself a nature which is infinitely lower than His own, even had He entered the world as a king clothed in purple and crowned with gold, would have been an immeasurable condescension. But for Him to be born a helpless infant entirely dependent on His mother, to be so poor as not to have a place where to lay His head, to have His life immediately sought after by a cruel king and His parents made fugitives from the wrath of this king, was in itself an act of condescension in our behalf utterly beyond anything that our minds can grasp. As He grew up He accomodated Himself to the limitations of human existence. Though He was the Giver of the Law, He submitted to circumcision, took His place under the Law as if He were an ordinary Israelite, and assumed its obligation in man's place and stead. As the Lutheran theologian, Dr. Joseph Stump, has observed: "His home was in the humble and despised village of Nazareth, amid rough and uncouth neighbors, in a narrow and contracted environment, and in the deepest obscurity. . . . Though Lord of all, He was subject to Joseph and Mary like an ordinary child of men, labored at the carpenter's bench, and subjected Himself to the hardships and limitations of the poor and lowly. . . . His public ministry brought Him into contact with all sorts of men, the best of whom were weak and sinful, and the worst of whom were quite depraved. Though divine and holy, He associated with them day by day as if He were simply one of them. He mingled with all kinds and classes of people, and dined with despised publicans and with self-righteous Pharisees. He was often hungry and thirsty, had no place to lay His head, like the lowest of them, and endured bitter hostility and persecution at the hands of the ruling classes of the Jews."[1]

While the humiliation and suffering of Jesus continued in greater or lesser degree throughout the whole period of His earthly life, it increased in intensity as His career neared its close. The opposition and hatred of His enemies became more intense. The indifference and callousness of the people, as well as the dreadful doom which He foresaw coming upon the whole Jewish nation—the nation to which He belonged and which He loved—weighed heavily upon Him. But the climax was reached as He endured the shameful suffering and death by crucifixion, which is the most horrible and agonizing form of death that has ever been invented by

---
1. *The Christian Faith*, p. 168. (Muhlenberg Press)

man. Nor were the physical sufferings all that He had to endure on the cross. As the sin-offering for His people He was treated as if He were sinful in His own person. The Father's presence, of which He had been so conscious throughout His entire life, was now withdrawn, as was also the light of the sun. His sensitive soul was left to suffer alone and in violent conflict with the forces of evil which sought desperately on this last occasion to cause His downfall and defeat His redemptive work. The anguished cry, "My God, my God, why hast thou forsaken me?" is an indication of the extremity of His suffering. In the nature of the case we can understand but faintly what He endured as He hung there. But this we do know, that He who did no sin, and on whom death therefore had no claim, voluntarily took our place and suffered the penalty which was due to us and so made atonement for our sin. We shall not shift to the Jews of that day, nor to the Romans, the responsibility for His crucifixion, but penitently confess that in its broader aspects it was our sin as well as theirs that brought that suffering upon Him,—primarily that it was for the redeemed individually, regardless of what age they may live in, that He carried that burden.

The humiliation of Christ was completed in His burial, in which His sacred body was put away in the grave as if He shared the common end of men who died and are buried, whose bodies decay and cease to be. But His body was not given over to decay. Instead, three days later it was raised in a glorious resurrection.

XIV.

THE EXALTATION OF CHRIST

IN ANSWER to the question, "Whence consisteth Christ's exaltation?" the Shorter Catechism says: "Christ's exaltation consisteth in His rising again from the dead on the third day, in ascending up into heaven, in sitting at the right hand of God the Father, and in coming to judge the world at the last day."

In the first place it must be apparent to all that the exaltation of Christ, as well as His humiliation, relates not to His Divine nature, which is and always has been infinitely blessed and glorious, but only to His human nature. His divine nature is immutable, and therefore not capable of either increase or diminution. His humiliation was temporary. It began with His birth and was completed with His burial, and it can never be repeated. His exaltation is permanent. It began with His resurrection and ascension. It continues now as He sits at the right hand of God the Father and directs the affairs of His advancing kingdom. It will be more fully revealed when at the end of the world He comes in the glory of His Father and with the holy angels to judge the nations and to assign to each individual his eternal destiny.

The resurrection of Christ was not only the first step in His glorification. It was also one of the most important truths of the Gospel. For by this act Christ conquered death and came forth alive out of the tomb. It was the proof that His work of redemption had been fully successful, that He had made a complete conquest of death. It showed that His work had fully satisfied the demands of the law (the law which God established at the original creation, that the soul that committed sin should die), and that death therefore had no further hold on Him nor on any of those for whom He died. It proved further that He was what He claimed to be, the Son of God, equal with the Father, God manifested in the flesh. And since He suffered and died not for any sin of His own but as the federal head and representative of His people, His resurrection is the guarantee that at the appointed time His people who are vitally related to Him shall also be raised in a glorious resurrection. It means that the Gospel is true, that Satan has been finally and completely defeated, and that the triumph of life over death, of truth over error, of good over evil, and of happiness over misery, is forever assured. Paul set forth the real importance of the resurrection when he said: "If Christ hath not been raised, then is our preaching vain, your faith also is vain. . . . If Christ hath not been raised, your faith is vain; ye are yet in your sins. Then they also that are fallen asleep in Christ have perished. If we have only hoped in Christ in this life, we are of all men most pitiable. But now hath Christ been raised from the dead, the first-fruits of them that are asleep. For since by man came death, by man came also the resurrection from the dead. For as in Adam all die, so also in Christ shall all be made alive. But each in his own order: Christ the firstfruits; then they that are Christ's at His coming," I Cor. 15:14-23.

The first and most impressive result of the resurrection, and, in fact, we may say the strongest proof of the resurrection, was found in the complete transformation which took place in the minds and hearts of the disciples. Whereas after

The Exaltation of Christ 95

the crucifixion they were utterly disheartened and were on the point of losing faith in Christ as the Messiah, they then became firmly convinced that He had risen from the dead and that He was the Son of God, the promised Messiah, the Saviour of the world. From that time on nothing could shake them from that conviction. They went forth and preached everywhere, and showed themselves ready to suffer and die if need be for the Gospel. We know that some of them did lose their lives in the service of their Lord. Tradition tells us that most of them thus died.

The second step in the exaltation of Christ was His ascension. Mark records very briefly that after He had spoken with the disciples, "He was received up into heaven, and sat down at the right hand of God," 16:19, which is, of course, the position of honor and influence, of power and majesty. Luke says that "He led them (the disciples) out until they were over against Bethany: and He lifted up His hands, and blessed them. And it came to pass, while He blessed them, He departed from them, and was carried up into heaven," 24:50,51. But the fullest account of the Ascension is given in the book of Acts. After recording the last words of Christ to the disciples it adds: "And when He had said these things, as they were looking, He was taken up; and a cloud received Him out of their sight. And while they were looking steadfastly into heaven as He went, behold two men stood by them in white apparel; who also said, Ye men of Galilee, why stand ye looking into heaven? This Jesus who was received up from you into heaven, shall so come in like manner as ye have beheld Him going into heaven," 1:9-11.

Concerning these verses Dr. Hodge says: "It appears, (1) That the ascension of Christ was of His whole person. It was the Theanthropos, the Son of God, clothed in our nature, having a true body and a reasonable soul, who ascended. (2) That the ascension was visible. The disciples witnessed the whole transaction. They saw the person of Christ gradually rise from the earth and 'go up' until a cloud hid Him from their view. (3) It was a local transfer of His person from one place to another; from earth to heaven. Heaven is therefore a place. In what part of the universe it is located is not revealed. But according to the doctrine of Scripture it is a definite portion of space where God specially manifests His presence, and where He is surrounded by His angels (who not being infinite, cannot be ubiquitous), and by the spirits of the just made perfect."[1]

Heaven is Christ's home, His throne, His temple. The ascension was the counterpart of His descent to earth. In an earlier section we discussed His pre-existence, and have seen that He "came" or "was sent" on a specific mission of redemption. Having brought that work to a wholly successful conclusion He returned to His heavenly home. This world with its present load of sin is not suited for the Redeemer's abode in His state of exaltation, and will not become so until it has undergone its great process of regeneration so as to become a new heaven and a new earth.

Furthermore, since Christ has provided an objective atonement and so satisfied all of the legal requirements for His people, it was necessary that that work should be effectively applied by the Holy Spirit to those for whom it was intended. It is the Holy Spirit who regenerates the souls of men and prepares them fully for the heavenly abode. In order to accomplish this He enlightens them spiritually, induces faith and repentance, and brings them through the whole process of sanctification. Apart from His regenerating power men

---
1. *Systematic Theology*, II, p. 630.

would have remained in their sins for ever and Christ's work would have been in vain. But before the Holy Spirit could begin His work it was necessary that Christ return to the Father. "It is expedient for you that I go away; for if I go not away, the Comforter will not come unto you; but if I go, I will send Him unto you," John 16:7. To quote Dr. Hodge again, "The great blessing which the prophets predicted as characteristic of the Messianic period, was the effusion of the Holy Spirit. To secure that blessing for the Church His ascension was necessary. He was exalted to give repentance and the remission of sins; to gather His people from all nations and during all ages until the work was accomplished. His throne in the heavens was the proper place whence the work of saving men, through the merits of His death, was to be carried on."[2]

It may be well to point out further in this connection that God's dealing with men in this world embraces three distinct dispensations in which the peculiar work of one of the persons of the Trinity is predominant. In the eternal plan of God there was what we may call a division of labor among the different persons of the Trinity and a definite order of events to be followed. That of the Father came first. It had to do primarily with creation and with the government or providential control of all things. It extended through the entire Old Testament period and up until the birth of Jesus in Bethlehem. That of the Son had to do particularly with redemption. It began with His birth in Bethlehem and continued until the day of Pentecost. During that time He provided an objective atonement and fulfilled all of the legal requirements for His people so that they might be brought from their estate of sin and misery into a state of

---
2. *Systematic Theology*, II, p. 635.

salvation. That of the Holy Spirit had to do primarily with salvation or the application to the hearts of men of this atonement which was provided for them by Christ. This dispensation began with the day of Pentecost and extends until the end of the world. This, of course, does not mean that during the dispensation of any one member of the Trinity the other two were inactive, but only that in matters pertaining to salvation the different members of the Trinity perform different functions.

In connection with Christ's resurrection and ascension it may be well to point out that it is in the person of the risen and glorified Christ that we shall see God. It would seem to be impossible for us ever to see God the Father or God the Holy Spirit as distinct persons of the Trinity, for each is pure spirit and infinite as regards space. But we shall see God the Son in His resurrection body. Moreover, we should also remember that Christ Himself said: "I and the Father are one," John 10:30; "I am in the Father, and the Father in me," John 14:11; and, "He that hath seen me hath seen the Father," John 14:9.

The third step in the exaltation of Christ is His sitting at the right hand of God. From there He directs the affairs of His advancing kingdom and maintains its perfect schedule. In order that His mediatorial reign should be wholly successful it was necessary that He should be given absolute dominion. "All authority hath been given unto me in heaven and on earth," Matt. 28:18, said He as He commissioned the disciples for their task of world-wide evangelism. "He must reign till He hath put all enemies under His feet," said Paul; and then he added, "The last enemy that shall be abolished is death," I Cor. 15:25,26,—which means, of course, the complete subjugation of the forces of sin, since sin and sin alone is the cause of death. His disciples are commanded to go and "make disciples of all the nations," Matt. 28:19, claiming their people for the true God through baptism "in the name of the Father and of the Son and of the Holy Spirit." And the message to be proclaimed in this universal evangelism is, of course, the full-orbed Gospel,—"teaching them to observe all things whatsoever I have commanded you," Matt. 28:20. We shall have more to say about the mediatorial reign of Christ when we come to discuss the subject, "Christ as King."

The fourth and last step in the exaltation of Christ will be His coming again with power and great glory to be the final Judge of the entire world. He is then to appear in His resurrection body, surrounded by all the angels, and is to sit on the throne of His glory (Matt. 25:31); every eye is to see Him (Rev. 1:7), this same Jesus who while on earth was rejected by His own people and arraigned as a criminal at the bar of Pilate, who was unjustly condemned and crucified with malefactors. From His lips all men are to receive their final rewards or punishments. Then, with His mediatorial reign completed and crowned with complete success, He is to deliver up the kingdom to the Father and resume His original relation to the other Persons of the Trinity, sharing fully in the glory which He had with the Father before the world was, and, together with the Father and the Holy Spirit, He is to reign forever as King over the redeemed: "And when all things have been subjected unto Him, then shall the Son also Himself be subjected to Him that did subject all things unto Him, that God may be all in all," I Cor. 15:28.

This, then, is what we mean by the exaltation of Christ. And again we would remind our readers that it is not the divine nature but the human nature of Jesus that is exalted, that it was the man Jesus Christ who received a resurrection body, who ascended to heaven, who shares in the mediatorial reign, and who will be seen by all peoples when He comes again at the last day.

XV.

THE RELATION OF THE TWO NATURES IN CHRIST

IN THE Westminster Confession of Faith we find this very clear and complete statement concerning the person of Christ: "The Son of God, the second person in the Trinity, being very and eternal God, of one substance, and equal with the Father, did, when the fulness of time was come take upon Himself man's nature, with all the essential properties and common infirmities thereof, yet without sin: being conceived by the power of the Holy Ghost, in the womb of the Virgin Mary, of her substance. So that the two whole, perfect, and distinct natures, the Godhead and the manhood, were inseparably jointed together in one person, without conversion, composition, or confusion. Which person is very God and very man, yet one Christ, the only Mediator between God and man."[1]

Many of the critics have gone astray in their study of the person of Christ for no other reason than that they have based their conclusions on the assumption that He must be either Divine or human. That He might be both Divine and human seems never to have entered their minds. They are therefore confronted at the very outset with an irreconcilable dilemma, for the whole historical tradition testifies to a Divine-human Jesus, a Jesus who is intensely supernatural and yet who is possessed of a perfectly normal human nature. The tendency of these critics is to tear apart the natural and the supernatural elements in the Gospels, then to assign the

1. Chapter VIII, Section 2.

natural elements to a supposedly "earlier" or "historical" narrative while discounting the supernatural elements as "accretions" or "myths." Such criticism, however, is utterly illegitimate. It is based not on historical or textual criticism, which presents not a shred of evidence for a merely human Christ, but entirely on *a priori* reasoning. Specifically, it is based on the philosophical assumption that the supernatural is impossible.

The evidence that we have concerning the historical Jesus comes primarily from the New Testament and secondarily from the beliefs and practices of the early Christians. This evidence admittedly sets forth a Divine-human Jesus. It is abundant and is consistently maintained in the various sources. It bears on its face the marks of honesty and sincerity. To reject it in the interests of a merely human Jesus who may perchance fit in more harmoniously with the critic's personal notion of what is real or possible, when that notion has not the slightest scrap of historical evidence to support it, is certainly highhanded and inexcusable. Whether the supernatural is possible or not, either in the person of Jesus or in the world at large, is not a question of historical or textual criticism, — which criticism should deal impartially and exclusively with the text of the New Testament that has been handed down to us and which incidentally fully supports belief in the supernatural. It is rather a question of philosophical world-view, and cannot be disposed of by an arbitrary rejection of unwanted elements in the Gospel narratives. In this chapter it is our purpose to show that it is entirely reasonable to believe that the two natures which the Gospel narratives ascribe to Jesus did function in His person with perfect harmony, and that only such a two-natured person would be capable of providing salvation for mankind.

The Relation of the Two Natures in Christ 103

In the incarnation our Lord added to His divine nature, not another person (which would have given Him a double personality), but impersonal, generic human nature, so that He was and continues to be God and man, in two distinct natures and one person for ever. There is, to be sure, mystery here which we cannot explain. Probably the nearest analogy we have to it is that which is found in man's own being. Man is composed of two radically different substances,—an immaterial soul or spirit which is subject to mental and spiritual influences, and a material body which is subject to all of the physical and chemical and electrical forces which operate in the world about him. These two natures are not fused or mixed so as to produce a third which is different from either of the others, but exist side by side in perfect harmony with all of their distinct attributes. Each continues to obey the laws of its realm as definitely as if detached from the other. And as in man the soul is the dominant and controlling factor, so in Christ the divine nature is dominant and controlling. In man the attributes or peculiarities of either nature are the attributes or peculiarities of the person. What can be affirmed of either of his natures can be affirmed of the person. If his spirit is moral or immoral, happy or sorrowful, wise or foolish, or if his body weighs one hundred and fifty pounds, is tall or short, has blue eyes, suffers pain or is sick, we do not bother to point out to which nature it is that these things apply but simply say that he as a person has these qualities or experiences these things. It will be acknowledged that each of these qualities or conditions applies exclusively to one nature and not to the other. The soul cannot be wounded or burnt or made lame or deaf; nor can the body think, or be happy or sorrowful, or have a good conscience or suffer remorse. Yet what the man is or experiences in either nature he is or experiences as a person.

Hence in view of the fact that Christ has two natures, and depending on which nature we have in mind, it is proper to say that He is infinite or that He is finite, that He existed from eternity or that He was born in Bethlehem, that He was omniscient or that He was limited in knowledge. In His composite personality He was, on the other side, "of the seed of David according to the flesh," and on the other He was "declared to be (that is, proved to be) the Son of God with power, according to the Spirit of holiness, by the resurrection from the dead," Rom. 1:3,4. Consequently the Scriptures present Him as the son of David, yet David's Lord. He is born an infant, yet is the Ancient of Days. He is the son of Mary, yet at the same time God over all, blessed forever. He is weary with His journey, yet He upholds all things by the word of His power. He can do nothing without the Father, yet without Him was not anything made that hath been made. He is bone of our bone and flesh of our flesh, yet might readily have clung exclusively to His equality with God. He takes the form of a servant, yet His proper and natural form was the form of God. He increases in stature, yet is the same yesterday, today and for ever. He increases in wisdom, yet knows the Father perfectly. He is born under the law and keeps the law, yet in His own name He gives a new and more perfect law and proclaims Himself the Lord of the Sabbath and greater than the temple. His soul is troubled, yet He is the Prince of Peace. He goes to His death at the command of the Roman governor, yet He is the King of kings and Lord of lords. He is received up into heaven out of the sight of His disciples yet continues to be with them even to the end of the world. Hence the Gospel writers sometimes

The Relation of the Two Natures in Christ 105

present Him as Divine, sometimes as human,—not that we are to take the one and leave the other, but that we are to accept Him as a Divine-human person, incarnate Deity, whose whole earthly life was but an episode in the existence of a heavenly Being.

We have said that the two natures in Christ are so united that the attributes or peculiarities of either nature can be predicated of the person. And since we mean exactly the same person whether we call Him Jesus or Christ, God or man, the Son of God or the Son of Man, it is perfectly correct to say that Jesus was thirsty or that God was thirsty, that Jesus suffered or that God suffered, that Jesus took man's place on the cross and died for him or that God took man's place on the cross and died for him, provided, of course, that we keep in mind the particular nature through which the action is accomplished. In Scripture the attributes and powers of either nature are ascribed to the one Christ, and conversely the works and characteristics of the one Christ are ascribed to either of the natures in a way which can be explained only on the principle that these two natures were organically and indissolubly united in a single person. The Scriptures tell us, for instance, that sinful men "crucified the Lord of glory," I Cor. 2:8. Paul refers to "the Church of the Lord which He purchased with His own blood," Acts 20:28, and declares that "there is one God, one Mediator also between God and man, Himself man, Jesus Christ," I Tim. 2:5. John writes of "that which was from the beginning, that which we have heard, that which we have seen with our eyes, that which we beheld, and our hands handled, concerning the Word of life," I John 1:1, and in another place declares that "they shall look on Him whom they pierced," John 19:37. When Jesus asked, "What then if ye should behold the Son of Man ascending where He was before?" a term which had special reference to His human nature was used to designate the person when the thing referred to was true only of His divine nature.

The expression, "Mary, mother of God," used so repeatedly in the Roman Catholic Church, is usually offensive to Protestant ears. Yet there is a sense in which it is true, provided that we keep in mind that Mary was the mother not of His divine nature but only of His human nature. But since it is so likely to be misunderstood by uninformed listeners and lends itself so readily to the propagation of error its use would be better discontinued.

It was necessary that the Redeemer of mankind should be both human and Divine. It was necessary that He be human if He was really to take man's place and suffer and die, for Deity as such was not capable of that. And it was necessary that He should be Divine if His suffering and death were to have infinite value. Briefly, His humanity made His suffering possible, while His Deity gave it infinite value. Had He been only man He would have needed to have worked out salvation for Himself, and even though He had been sinless He could not have paid a ransom sufficient for the deliverance of others. But since He possessed two natures united in perfect harmony and was no less truly Divine than truly human, the atonement which He made was infinitely meritorious and therefore sufficient to save as many members of this fallen race as put their faith in Him. Furthermore, since the race fell through the action of one man who acted in his representative and official capacity, it was possible for salvation to be provided in the same way. As Calvin has so well expressed it, in order that man might be reconciled to God it was necessary "that man, who had ruined himself by his

The Relation of the Two Natures in Christ 107

own disobedience, should remedy his condition by obedience, should satisfy the justice of God, and suffer the punishment of his sin. Our Lord then made His appearance as a real man; He put on the character of Adam, and assumed his name, to act as his substitute in his obedience to the Father, to lay down our flesh as the price of satisfaction to the justice of God; and to suffer the punishment which we deserved, in the same nature in which the offense had been committed. As it would have been impossible, therefore, for one who was only God to suffer death, or for one who was a mere man to overcome it, He associated the human nature with the Divine, that He might submit the weakness of the former to death, as an atonement for sins; and that with the power of the latter He might contend with death, and obtain a victory on our behalf. Those who despoil Christ, therefore, either of His Divinity or His humanity either diminish His majesty and glory, or obscure His goodness."[2]

We have said that it was not with another man that the Second Person of the Trinity united Himself, but with impersonal generic human nature. This human nature had no personality apart from the Divine nature, but came to consciousness and found its personality only in union with the Divine, in much the same way that our physical bodies if separated from our spirits are devoid of all reason and sensation and are as nothing, but when united with our spirits they share our true personal life because we, whose bodies they are, are persons. In this union the Divine nature was basic and controlling, so that this was not the case of a man being exalted to Deity, but of God voluntarily humbling Himself and descending to the plane of man in such a manner that He shared equally with us the experiences which are

---
2. *Institutes*, I, 421.

common to men. In the same manner that our spirits take precedence over and control our bodies, the Divine nature in Christ took precedence over and controlled the human; yet each nature continued to have its own distinctive attributes or properties and to fulfill its own functions.

Incidentally, the fact that Christ took into union with Himself not another person but impersonal generic human nature throws considerable light on the problem of His immaculate conception by the Virgin Mary. It has often been asked how Christ could be born a member of the human race and yet be free from original sin. But the fact of the matter is that sin and guilt are attached not to human nature as such, but to individual persons,—specifically to all who are sons of Adam by ordinary generation. Furthermore, had Jesus been born not of a virgin but of a human father and mother there would have been some reason for believing that it was a complete human being which He took into union with Himself. In the realm of the human it requires both a father and a mother to produce a new being possessing body and soul. But since Jesus had only a human mother He could have taken into union with His Divine nature not a human person but only impersonal human nature, in which nature, however, He was able to experience all of the limitations and sufferings which are common to men. Hence the entail of original sin which rests upon all other members of the human race had no hold on Him. This consideration also shows how unnecessary and even ridiculous is the Roman Catholic doctrine of the immaculate conception of the Virgin Mary as an explanation of the sinlessness of Christ's nature.

In treating of the two natures of Christ we must ever keep in mind the unity of His person. Though as truly God as is God the Father and as truly man as we are, in the New Testa-

The Relation of the Two Natures in Christ

ment records He invariably speaks of Himself and is spoken of as but a single personality. Never are the pronouns "I," "thou," or "He," used to distinguish between the Divine and human nature as is done to distinguish between the different persons of the Trinity, and never does Christ use the plural number in referring to Himself. The distinction seems to lie in the fact that the different members of the Godhead have distinct (that is, individual) subsistence with powers of consciousness and will, but that the human nature of Christ does not and is therefore of itself not a distinct personality. Throughout the New Testament Jesus is presented as a Divine person living and moving in the flesh. It is but one and the same person of whom birth, growth, life, death, eternity, omniscience, omnipotence, and all the other attributes, whether human or Divine, are predicated. For any one to pick out certain statements in that tradition which emphasize the humanity of Jesus and on the basis of those to represent Him as merely human, is as erroneous as to pick out certain other statements which emphasize His Divinity and to represent Him as purely Divine. And for any one to confound the two natures so that they are merged into a third which is neither Divine nor human (as was the heresy of the Eutychians—condemned by the Council of Chalcedon, 451 A.D.), or to separate the two natures so as to give Christ a double personality (which was the heresy of the Nestorians —condemned by the Council at Ephesus, 431 A.D.), is equally erroneous. Each of these errors has tended to crop up time and again, and can be disposed of only through a correct understanding of His person.

This doctrine of the two natures united in one person is found to be the key which unlocks all of the treasures of Biblical instruction concerning the person of Christ and enables the reader to arrange the Scripture declarations into a fully intelligent and consistent system. It is inconceivable that the key which unlocks such a complicated lock can fail to be the true key. As Dr. Warfield has said concerning this doctrine: "The doctrine of the Two Natures supplies, in a word, the only possible solution of the enigmas of the life-manifestation of the historical Jesus. It presents itself to us, not as the creator, but as the solvent of difficulties—in this, performing the same service to thought which is performed by all the Christian doctrines. If we look upon it merely as a hypothesis, it commands our attention by the multiplicity of phenomena which it reduces to order and unifies, and on this lower ground, too, commends itself to our acceptance. But it does not come to us merely as a hypothesis. It is the assertion concerning their Lord of all the primary witnesses of the Christian faith. It is, indeed, the self-testimony of our Lord Himself, disclosing to us the mystery of His being. It is, to put it briefly, the simple statement of 'the fact of Jesus, as that fact is revealed to us in His whole manifestation. We may reject it if we will, but in rejecting it we reject the only real Jesus in favor of another Jesus—who is not another, but is the creature of pure fantasy. The alternatives which we are really face to face with are, Either the two-natured Christ of history, or—a strong delusion."[3]

And in another connection the same writer says concerning the New Testament portrait of Jesus that it is "the portrait not of a merely human life, though it includes the delineation of a complete and completely human life. It is the portrayal of a human episode in the divine life. It is, therefore, not merely connected with supernatural occurences, nor merely colored by supernatural features, nor merely set in a

---
3. *Christology and Criticism*, p. 309.

The Relation of the Two Natures in Christ

supernatural atmosphere: the supernatural is its very substance, the elimination of which would be the evaporation of the whole. The Jesus of the New Testament is not fundamentally man, however divinely gifted: He is God tabernacling for a while among men, with heaven lying about Him not merely in His infancy, but throughout all the days of His flesh.

"The intense supernaturalism of this portraiture is, of course, an offense to our anti-supernaturalistic age. It is only what was to be expected, therefore, that throughout the last century and a half a long series of scholars, imbued with the anti-supernaturalistic instinct of the time, have assumed the task of desupernaturalizing it. Great difficulty has been experienced, however, in the attempt to construct a historical sieve which will strain out miracles and yet let Jesus through; for Jesus is Himself the greatest miracle of them all. Accordingly at the end of the day there is a growing disposition, as if in despair of accomplishing this feat, to construct a sieve so as to strain out Jesus too; to take refuge in the council of desperation which affirms that there never was such a person as Jesus, that Christianity had no founder, and that not merely the portrait of Jesus but Jesus Himself, is a pure projection of later ideals into the past. The main stream of assault still addresses itself, however, to the attempt to eliminate not Jesus Himself, but the Jesus of the Evangelists, and to substitute for Him a desupernaturalized Jesus."[4]

Throughout the whole study of the relationship which exists between the two natures we are, of course, face to face with impenetrable mystery. It is one of those mysteries which the Scriptures reveal but which they make no effort to explain. Christ is an absolutely unique person; and although

---
4. *Christology and Criticism*, p. 163.

in every age much study has been expended upon His personality it remains a profound mystery, in some respects as baffling as the Trinity itself. All we can know are the simple facts which are revealed to us in Scripture, and beyond these it is not necessary to go. As a matter of fact we do not understand the mysterious union of the spiritual and physical in our own natures; nor do we understand the attributes of God. But the essential facts are clear and are understandable by the average Christian. These are that the Second Person of the Trinity added to His own nature a perfectly normal human nature, that His life on earth was passed as far as was fitting within the limits of this humanity, that His life remained at all times the life of God manifest in the flesh, that His action in the flesh never escaped beyond the boundary of that which was suitable for incarnate Deity, and that all of this was done in order that in man's nature and as man's Substitute He might assume man's obligation before the law, suffer the penalty which was due to him for sin, and so accomplish his redemption.

XVI.

THE INCARNATION

IN ANSWER to the question, "How did Christ, being the Son of God, become man?" the Shorter Catechism replies: "Christ, the Son of God, became man, by taking to Himself a true body and a reasonable (that is, reasoning) soul, being conceived by the power of the Holy Ghost, in the womb of the Virgin Mary, and born of her, yet without sin."

Man, in contrast with all of the animals of the field, was created in the image of God, with a spiritual and rational nature, and was given an immortal soul. Paul says that God is "not far from each one of us," and that "in Him we live, and move, and have our being," Acts 17:27, 28. The divine and the human, though distinct from each other, are not foreign to each other or mutually exclusive. Man is, as it were, a spark out of the great fire, or, to change the figure, he is an empty vessel to be filled from the infinite Fountain, and fulfills his appointed purpose only when in union with the divine. Since he was created in the image of God and was appointed a ruler in the earth he is in effect a minature God. This, too, is in harmony with Scripture, for in Ps. 82:6 we read, "I said, Ye are gods, And all of you sons of the Most High;" and Christ Himself said, "Is it not written in your law, I said, Ye are gods?" John 10:34. Hence a union between the Divine and the human, while not inherently necessary, and while in all probability it would never have been made apart from God's work of redemption, was very definitely within the realm of possibility, and, given

God's desire to rescue man from sin, is seen to have been a most natural and effective method of procedure. "God may assume the form of man," says Dr. J. Ritchie Smith, "because man was made in the likeness of God. The Eternal Word may become the Son of Man because man is by nature the son of God. He could not take upon Him a nature wholly foreign to His own, nor become that which is altogether unlike Himself."

The incarnation was not an end in itself, but a means toward that end. Since man by his fall into sin had cut himself off from God and made himself utterly incapable of working out his own salvation, Christ in His infinite mercy assumed that task for him. It was for that purpose that He became incarnate, so that, as God dwelling in a human body, God clothed in human flesh, He might assume man's place before the law and satisfy Divine justice. Only a truly human person could suffer and die, and only a truly Divine person could give that suffering infinite value. The ultimate end of Our Lord's incarnation is therefore declared to be that He might die. "Since then the children are sharers in flesh and blood, He also Himself in like manner partook of the same; that through death He . . might deliver all them who through fear of death were all their lifetime subject to bondage . . . Wherefore it behooved Him in all things to be made like unto His brethren, that He might become a merciful and faithful high priest in things pertaining to God, to make propitiation for the sins of the people," Heb. 2:14-17.

The doctrine of the Deity of Christ is, of course, not dependent on the doctrine of the Incarnation. As Dr. J. Gresham Machen has pointed out, "The doctrine of the Deity of Christ is part of the Biblical teaching about God. This person whom we know as Jesus Christ would have been God

The Incarnation

even if no universe had been created and even if there had been no fallen man to save. He was God from everlasting. His Deity is quite independent of any relation of His to a created world. The doctrine of the incarnation, on the other hand, is part of the doctrine of salvation. He *was* from everlasting, but He *became* man—at a definite moment in the world's history, and in order that fallen man might be saved. That He became man was not at all necessary to the unfolding of His own being. He was infinite, eternal and unchangeable God when He became man and after He became man. But He would have been infinite, eternal and unchangeable God, even if He had never become man. His becoming man was a free act of His love. Ultimately its purpose, as the purpose of all things, was the glory of God; and that purpose does not conflict at all with the fact that it was a free act of mercy to undeserving sinners. He became man in order that He might die on the cross to redeem sinners from the guilt and power of sin."[1]

Paul's doctrine of the Incarnation is perhaps expressed most fully in Phil. 2:5-11, where he refers to Christ as "existing in the form of God," and as "taking the form of a servant, being made in the likeness of men, and being found in fashion as a man." Numerous other allusions are found throughout his epistles. In II Cor. 8:9, for instance, we are reminded of the graciousness of "Our Lord Jesus Christ, who, though He was rich, yet for our sakes became poor, that we through His poverty might become rich." In Gal. 4:4 we are told that "When the fulness of the time came, God sent forth His Son, born of a woman, born under the law, that He might redeem them that were under the law, that we might receive the adoption of sons."

---

1. Article in *The Presbyterian Guardian*.

Concerning the statement in Gal. 4:4 Dr. Warfield makes the following comment: "The whole transaction is referred to the Father in fulfillment of His eternal plan of redemption, and it is described specifically as an incarnation: the Son of God is born of a woman—He who is in His own nature the Son of God, abiding with God, is sent forth from God in such a manner as to be born a human being, subject to law." (i.e., the ceremonial law). "The primary implications are that this was not the beginning of His being; but that before this He was neither a man nor subject to law. But there is no suggestion that on becoming man and subject to law, He ceased to be the Son of God or lost anything intimated by that high designation." And then concerning this general subject he continues: "Paul teaches us that by His coming forth from God to be born of a woman, Our Lord, assuming a human nature to Himself, has, while remaining the Supreme God, become also true and perfect man. Accordingly, in a context in which the resources of language are strained to the utmost to make the exaltation of Our Lord's being clear—in which He is described as the image of the invisible God, whose being antedates all that is created, in whom, through whom and to whom all things have been created, and in whom they all subsist—we are told not only that (naturally) in Him all the fulness dwells (Col. 1:19), but, with concrete explication, that 'all the fulness of the Godhead dwells in Him bodily' (Col. 2:9); that is to say, the very Deity of God, that which makes God God, in all its completeness, has its permanent home in Our Lord, and that in a 'bodily fashion,' that is, it is in Him clothed with a body. He who looks upon Jesus Christ sees, no doubt, a body and a man; but as he sees the man clothed with the body, so he sees God Himself, in all the fulness of His Deity, clothed with humanity. Jesus Christ is therefore God 'manifested in the flesh' (I Tim.

3:16), and His appearance on earth is an 'epiphany' (II Tim. 1:10), which is the technical term for manifestations on earth of a God. Though truly man, He is nevertheless also our 'great God' (Titus 2:13)."[2]

The incarnation not only made it possible for God to provide redemption for man. It made possible a much fuller revelation of God to men, which in turn meant that His truth and ideals would become the ruling principles in the inner life of an ever-increasing number of men down through the ages. During the Old Testament dispensation God spoke to the people through the prophets, revealing to them something of His own nature, of man's sinful and lost condition, and of the plan of salvation. But the glory of the present dispensation is that in Christ God *came personally*, and through His own person and work has given man an incomparably more advanced revelation concerning both His own nature and the plan of salvation. "When men looked upon Jesus," said Dr. Machen, "they actually saw with their eyes one who was truly God. That is the marvel of the incarnation. To behold with one's bodily eyes one who was truly God—what greater wonder can there possibly be than this?"

We may say further that Christ is the final and perfect revelation of God to men, and that He will continue to be such not only on this earth but also in heaven. For while we dare not speak with assurance concerning mysteries so high, yet it seems inconceivable that God in His essential nature as an infinite Spirit can ever be seen by men either in this world or in the next. He it is "whom no man hath seen, nor can see," I Tim. 6:16. But in Christ the Infinite Spirit manifests Himself in finite, human form, that the creature may

---
2. *Biblical Doctrines*, p. 383.

apprehend Him. We have said that it would seem that even in heaven our vision of God will be that of Christ in His glorified body, which will be finite and limited to one particular place,—not that His body will always remain in the same place, but that it, like our own resurrection bodies, will be in only one place at a time. It is well to remember that the book of Revelation repeatedly pictures Christ on the throne in heaven, and that it is before His throne that the redeemed sing their praises and give thanks for the marvelous deliverance that has been provided for them. We shall then see God in Christ; but apparently we shall not see God the Father nor God the Holy Spirit as such, but only know of their presence through their love for us and their influence over us. Assuming this to be true, the Lord Jesus Christ stands out all the more clearly as the final and perfect revelation of God to men.

It should be observed that as Christ entered into this vital, personal relationship with human nature He conferred upon it an inestimable blessing in that our nature was taken, as it were, into the very bosom of Deity. It was thereby lifted far above that of the angels. With no other creatures in the entire universe does He sustain such a close and intimate relation. As the writer of the Epistle to the Hebrews says, "Since then the children are sharers in flesh and blood, He also Himself in like manner partook of the same. . . . For verily not to angels doth He give help, but He giveth help to the seed of Abraham," 2:14-16. Furthermore, the human nature which Jesus assumed in the incarnation is His forever. He brought it with Him when He rose from the grave and with it He returned to the Father. In heaven He appeared to John like unto a Son of Man, in human form, Rev. 1:13; and the dying Stephen saw the Son of Man stand-

The Incarnation

ing on the right hand of God, the position of honor and power, Acts 7:56. Through the resurrection and the further exaltation of Christ human nature has in truth attained to the very throne of the universe.

The sojourn of Christ on earth was therefore not a mere theophany or temporary appearance of God in human form, but a real and permanent incarnation. Various Old Testament persons had seen theophanies: Abraham (Gen. 18:1-33); Jacob (Gen. 32:24-30); Moses (Ex. 24:9-11; 34:5, 6); Joshua (Josh. 5:13-15); the father and mother of Sampson (Ju. 13:2-22); Isaiah (Is. 6:1-5); Daniel's three friends (Dan. 3:24, 25); etc. But the incarnation of Christ was quite different. In the incarnation God was born a babe in Bethlehem. For a period of thirty-three years that union continued in a form which manifested the human much more clearly than the Divine, although on numerous occasions the Divine made itself manifest through supernatural works. Particularly on the mount of transfiguration the veil was partially removed and the Divine showed out in its true glory. But with the resurrection and ascension human nature, by virtue of its union with Deity, was glorified far beyond anything of which it was capable in this world.

Concerning the probability or improbability that there would be an incarnation, and the amount of evidence that would be required to convince the average person that an incarnation had taken place, Dr. Craig makes the following worthwhile comment: "We all know that the amount of evidence required to produce faith in an event varies with the nature of the event itself. If, for instance, one or two persons of ordinary veracity should tell you that they had seen a man knocked down by an automobile you would no doubt believe them, since there is nothing very improbable about such an event. If, however, twelve of the most intelligent and upright men of this community should tell you that they had seen a man with the feet of a dog and the wings of a bird, it is not probable that you would believe them. In the one case you would believe on very slight evidence; in the other you would refuse to believe in the face of exceedingly strong evidence. It is not surprising, therefore, that men should admit that the evidence in favor of the Incarnation is strong and yet that they should refuse to admit that such an event ever took place."

And then he continues: "Now, is there such an antecedent presumption against the Incarnation as these would have us believe? I do not think so. In fact, I maintain that when this event is looked at in the light of its purpose we are warranted in saying rather that the presumption is in favor of its occurrence. At this point everything hinges, so it seems to me, upon the moral and spiritual condition of this world. If we think that this world is, on the whole, in a normal condition, morally and spiritually; that men do not stand in any real need of a Saviour from the guilt and power of sin, we will think it more or less inconceivable that God's Son should have assumed flesh and dwelt among us—because we will be unable to perceive that there was any real need for such an act on His part. But if, on the other hand, we believe that this world is in an abnormal condition, morally and spiritually; that it has gone wrong, seriously wrong, so wrong that it is a lost and condemned world; then for those who believe in the existence of a God who is interested in the welfare of His creatures, the presumption is in favor of the notion that He will intervene, that He will put forth His hand to save and to redeem."

"I hold, therefore, that the credibility of the Incarnation is bound up with the question of the moral and spiritual

The Incarnation

condition of mankind. I am not alone in this. Men in general hold with me in this, as is evident from the fact that we find a close connection between men's views of the moral and spiritual condition of the race and their attitude toward the Incarnation. Generally speaking, where we find men thinking that there isn't much the matter with this world, or at least that it is in as good condition as we can fairly expect at this stage of its development, we find men who refuse to believe in Christ as God manifest in the flesh; but where we find men who recognize that this is a lost world, a world that left to itself would fester in its corruption from eternity to eternity, there we find men who perceive the need of an Incarnation and so men who are ready to assign due weight to the evidence that goes to show that God did indeed so love this world that He gave His only-begotten Son that whosoever believeth in Him might not perish but have eternal life."[3]

The importance of the doctrine of the Incarnation in the Christian system can hardly be over-estimated, for the integrity of Christianity as the redemptive religion divinely set forth stands or falls with this doctrine. Nowhere is this more clearly stated than in the First Epistle of John which, written late in the life of the Apostle and at a time when many had begun to apostatize and deny the faith, was designed primarily to establish the faith of believers in the midst of widespread errors. Chief of these errors was the denial, in one form or other, of the incarnation of the Son of God. John not only insists strenuously on the acknowledgment that Jesus Christ has come in the flesh, but makes this the fundamental doctrine of the Gospel. "Every spirit that confesseth that Jesus Christ is come in the flesh," says he,

---
3. *Jesus As He Was and Is*, p. 62.

"is of God; and every spirit that confesseth not Jesus is not of God: and this is the spirit of the antichrist, whereof ye have heard that it cometh; and now it is in the world already," I John 4:2, 3. "Whosoever believeth that Jesus is the Christ is begotten of God. . . . And who is he that overcometh the world, but he that believeth that Jesus is the Son of God? . . . He that hath the Son hath life; he that hath not the Son of God hath not the life. . . . We know that the Son of God is come, and hath given us an understanding, that we know Him that is true, and we are in Him that is true, even in His Son Jesus Christ. This is the true God, and eternal life." I John 5:1-20. Judged by this infallible touchstone Modernism, Unitarianism, Christian Science, and all other systems which deny the Deity of Christ or His incarnation stand condemned as false religions.

XVII.

THE SINLESSNESS OF JESUS

IN ANY study of the person of Christ it is important to keep in mind that He was altogether free from sin. The Apostle Peter, who had occasion to know Him well, describes Him as "the Holy One of God," John 6:69, and affirms that He "did no sin, neither was guile found in His mouth," I Peter 2:22. The Apostle John declares that "In Him is no sin," I John 3:5. The writer of the Epistle to the Hebrews says that He was "holy, guiltless, undefiled, separated from sinners," 7:26, that He was "in all points tempted like as we are, yet without sin," 4:15, and that He "through the eternal Spirit offered Himself without blemish unto God," 9:14. Paul's witness is that He "knew no sin," II Cor. 5:21. The angel Gabriel, in announcing to Mary that she was to become the mother of Jesus, said, "The holy thing which is begotten shall be called the Son of God," Luke 1:35.

Various other sources also testify to the sinlessness of Jesus. The traitor Judas, smitten with remorse, declared, "I have sinned in that I betrayed innocent blood," Matt. 27:4. Pilate's wife warned her husband, "Have thou nothing to do with that righteous man," Matt. 27:19. Pilate weakly proclaimed the innocence of Jesus when he washed his hands before the multitude, saying, "I am innocent of the blood of this righteous man," Matt. 27:24. One of the thieves who was crucified with Him said, "We receive the due reward of our deeds: but this man hath done nothing amiss," Luke 23:41. And the Roman centurion who witnessed the death of Jesus said, "Truly this was the Son of God," Matt. 27:54.

But most important of all in establishing His sinlessness is the testimony of Jesus himself. "I do always the things that are pleasing to Him," John 8:29. "The prince of the world cometh: and he hath nothing in me," John 14:30. To His enemies, the very ones who were most anxious to point out some flaw in His character, He threw out the challenge, "Which of you convicteth me of sin?" John 8:46,—and the challenge went unanswered. As He stood within the shadow of the cross and reviewed His life He could find no failure of duty, no stain upon His life: "I have kept my Father's commandments," John 15:10; and again, "I have glorified thee on the earth, having accomplished the work which thou gavest me to do," John 17:4. Nowhere in the records do we find that Jesus ever betrayed the slightest consciousness of sin. He prayed often, but never for pardon. He prayed, "Father, forgive them," Luke 23:34, and taught His disciples to pray, "Forgive us our debts," Matt. 6:12; but never does He pray, "Father, forgive me." He went often to the temple, but never offered sacrifice (the essential principle behind sacrifice being, as we are taught in the Old Testament, to acknowledge one's sin and propitiate offended Deity). Death was for Him not the wages of sin, but a voluntary sacrifice for the sake of others. Free both from hereditary depravity and from actual sin, He carried morality to the highest point attained or even attainable by humanity. In His own person He presented the rare spectacle of a life uniformly noble and consistent with His own lofty principles, so that in the Christian religion His own conduct has become the ideal which all of His followers seek to imitate. No other teacher has ever approximated the standards of

The Sinlessness of Jesus 125

Jesus, and both friend and foe are almost unanimous in acknowledging His moral grandeur. It was, of course, necessary that the One who was to redeem the world should Himself be free from sin; for no one who was a sinner and who therefore had forfeited his own life could atone for others.

Jesus' claim to sinlessness, and the serenity of His moral and spiritual life, are all the more impressive when we remember that, (1) He was a Jew, trained in the Old Testament with its strong emphasis on the holiness of God and the sinfulness of all men,—compare, for instance, the words of the pious Jew as expressed by Peter when the centurion Cornelius attempted to worship him: "Stand up; I myself also am a man," Acts 10:26; or the words of Paul when the multitude at Lystra would have worshipped him and Barnabas: "We also are men of like passions with you," Acts 14:15. (2) He was keenly conscious of the prevalence and power of sin, and quick to detect it in others. (3) He more than any other teacher pointed out the spiritual meaning of the law as it related to the inner life, motives and character of men. (4) Self-righteousness was to Him the most abhorrent and the most strongly condemned of sins. And, (5) the holiest among the saints of earth have been most conscious of their unworthiness and most sensible of their sin. Certainly throughout His teaching and the general mode of His life, including the working of many miraculous cures and works of mercy, Jesus acts precisely as we would expect incarnate Deity to act.

As a matter of fact, it was impossible for Christ to commit sin. For in His essential nature He was God, and God cannot sin. This does not mean that He could not be tempted; for as the writer of the Epistle to the Hebrews says, "We have not a High Priest that cannot be touched with the feeling of our infirmities; but one that hath been in all points tempted like as we are, yet without sin," 4:15. In order for us to understand how Christ could have been tempted while at the same time there was no possibility that He would fall it is necessary that we keep in mind the real nature of temptation. This has been well expressed by the Lutheran theologian, Dr. Joseph Stump, who says: "Temptation is literally a testing, to see whether the tested one will choose God's service or not. This does not necessarily imply the possibility of a failure to stand the test. Gold may be tested as well as dross. And gold can never fail to stand the test. Theoretically, that is, as long as we do not know that the metal in question is gold, there may be the possibility in our minds that it will fail when put to the proof. But actually there is no such possibility. The gold, just because it is gold, will stand the test and cannot possibly fail to do so. If we were in ignorance of the true nature of Christ's person, we should suppose that He might have failed in the hour of temptation. But knowing, as we do, that He is the veritable Son of God, we know that He could not have sinned. Being pure gold, He could not fail to stand the test. He might be tempted by Satan in many ways; but it was not possible that He should fall, because He was the Son of God."[1]

Since Christ was free from every taint of either inherited or personal sin, there was nothing in Him to which sin could appeal, nothing to which it could commend itself as attractive. This was the meaning of the words, "The prince of the world cometh; and he hath nothing in me," John 14:30. The Devil could find not the slightest evil tendency or desire in the personality of Jesus to which he could make an appeal, no basis on which He could be persuaded to accomplish His

---

1. *The Christian Faith*, p. 148.

The Sinlessness of Jesus

ends by other than lawful means. Since His Divine nature was the dominant and controlling principle in His personality, His human will, which was always in full harmony with His Divine will, was kept steadily inclined toward the right. Consequently, sin, regardless of the form in which it was presented, was always repulsive to Him. Sin often does seem attractive to us and we become its victim, because we still have remnants of the old sinful nature clinging to us, although happily we do find some persons who have made such progress in the Christian way that sin is practically always repulsive to them. And if in this life we find that some of those who have been redeemed reach a state in which they almost invariably turn from sin with contempt, it is not strange that the holy nature of Jesus, which was entirely free from all mental and moral aberrations and from all inherited and personal sin, should unerringly have rejected all temptations to do evil. Christ's inability to commit sin was, strictly speaking, not a limitation, but a perfection; for certainly there is no surer proof of imperfection than that when confronted with a choice between good and evil the person is capable of choosing evil. Consequently, one of the rewards that we look forward to in heaven is that of being confirmed in holiness so that we too shall be unable to commit sin.

XVIII.

THE VIRGIN BIRTH

IN THE opening chapters of Matthews's and of Luke's Gospel we are given an account of the virgin birth of Jesus. This miracle has been the occasion for considerable debate both within and without the Church, and has often served as a kind of touchstone to indicate whether or not a person is an evangelical. As a general rule one who accepts the virgin birth as true will also accept the other miraculous elements in Scripture, while one who rejects it will also reject a considerable portion of the other miracles. It is therefore of more than average importance, not only because of its bearing on the doctrine of the person of Christ, but also because of its representative character.

We are frequently told nowadays that the presumption is altogether against the notion that miracles should have happened, since they involve a break in the order of nature. If we take into consideration only the physical world the presumption against miracles is, no doubt, almost overwhelming; for it is very evident that we live in an ordered world in which events are casually connected and in which there is no place for chance or caprice. So far as ordinary events are concerned the reign of natural law is invariable. The redemption of mankind, however, is not an ordinary, but a most extraordinary event. In fact, since it is something which determines our eternal condition for happiness or misery we cannot conceive of an event more extraordinary.

The Virgin Birth 129

If we take into consideration moral and spiritual values and grant that the human race is in a very abnormal condition morally and spiritually—that it has, in fact, gone so seriously wrong that if left to itself its condition would be hopeless—the whole matter assumes a different aspect. The presumption then becomes strongly in favor of the view that a loving and merciful God would intervene for the salvation of His people; and such intervention, in the very nature of the case, would involve the miraculous. Miracles then are seen, not as isolated wonders or prodigies for the occurrence of which no good reason can be given, but organically related events in a great system of redemption, at the very center of which stands Christ Himself. Hence the miracles recorded in both the Old and the New Testament, and particularly the miracles of the incarnation and the Resurrection, have to do not with things trivial but with things supremely important. Granted that Christ is the supernatural person that we believe Him to be, it was most appropriate that His entrance into the world and His exit from the world should have been accompanied and accredited by manifestations of the supernatural. Hence the question whether or not miracles have occurred turns on the question whether or not God has provided redemption for His people; and to scoff at the miraculous is to scoff at the reality of redemption.

By way of background for a discussion of the virgin birth it may be well to remind ourselves of the general circumstances which attended that event. These have been set forth beautifully and logically in the following paragraph by Dr. George T. Purves: "Joseph was a carpenter by trade, a man of humble station though of high descent, and a devout Israelite. To Mary the angel announced that she was to become the mother of Messiah (Luke 1:28-38) by the power of the Holy Spirit working in her, and that the child, who was to be called Jesus, should have the throne of His father David. . . . Joseph, seeing her condition, was disposed quietly to put her away without public accusation, but even this gentle treatment was forestalled. An angel revealed to Him in a dream the cause of Mary's condition; told him that he was to have Messiah for his child; and that, as Isaiah had foretold, the latter was to be born of a virgin. With faith, equal to Mary's, Joseph believed the message and made Mary his legal wife. It was thus secured that Mary's child was born of a virgin, and at the same time that He had a legal human father and His mother protected by the love and respectability of a husband. . . . The narrative of Christ's birth beautifully harmonizes with what we now know of His dignity and His mission upon earth. The Messiah was to be the perfect flower of Israel's spiritual life; and so Jesus was born in the bosom of this pious family circle where the pure religion of the Old Testament was believed and cherished. The Messiah was to appear in lowliness; and so Jesus came from the home of the Nazarene carpenter. The Messiah was to be the son of David, and so Joseph, His legal father, and probably Mary, His actual mother, were descendants from David. The Messiah was to be the incarnation of God, a Divine Person uniting to Himself a human nature, and so Jesus was born of a woman but miraculously conceived by the power of the Holy Spirit."[2]

As a matter of fact, it is just in proportion as men lose their sense of the Divine personality of Christ that they come to doubt the reality or the necessity of the virgin birth. If we believe that He existed as God before He came to earth,

---
2. *Davis Bible Dictionary*, p. 382.

that His birth was heralded by the appearance of a star and by the anouncement of the angels to the shepherds, and that miracles constantly attended His public ministry and were especially conspicuous at the time of His death, resurrection and ascension, then the virgin birth will seem but the natural and normal things in the event of such a person. A natural birth would have been a most unnatural thing for such a person as Jesus. Grant the Deity of Christ, and all trouble concerning miracles vanishes away. It then becomes easy to accept all that the Gospels record concerning Him. It is then seen as entirely appropriate that this miraculous life should have been bounded on the one side by the virgin birth and on the other by the resurrection and the ascension. It would, indeed, have been strange and incredible if Deity had entered the human race any other way. There is, in fact, nothing about His person which is not unusual. He Himself is the great miracle, and we expect Him to move in the atmosphere of the supernatural where both His person and His message can be accredited by indisputable proofs. The miracles then become the reasonable thing, not the unreasonable; the credible, not the incredible. In proportion as the Christianity of the New Testament remains vivid and vital to men they instinctively feel that the virgin birth alone is consistent with the person and work of Christ, that He should acknowledge no other father than the Father who is in heaven, from whom alone He came forth to save the world. In fact, had His birth been otherwise we should have felt instinctively that something was amiss. Had He had an ordinary birth with a human father a strong discordant note would have been struck which would have thrown all of the other elements out of tune, and an invitation would thereby have been given for the world to have conceived of the supernatural Saviour as but a natural man. "Born into our race

He might be and was; but born of our race, never—whether really or only apparently," says Dr. Warfield.

The close connection between the Deity of Christ and the accounts concerning the virgin birth as given in the Gospels of Matthew and Luke is clearly expressed in the following paragraphs by Dr. Craig. Says he: "Are we to regard these accounts as sober statements of truth, or are we to place them on a par with the mythological tales of a somewhat similar nature that meet us in other connections? Assuredly our reply cannot be made without reference to the question whether the life and career of Jesus stamp Him as a divine being. If I believe that there was nothing in His life and career inconsistent with my regarding Him as a mere man, *i.e.*, one who was wholly the product of the forces ordinarily energizing in this world, I might not esteem the story of the virgin birth credible. In that case I might feel certain not only that He had a human mother but that He had a human father like the rest of us, and look upon the accounts of Matthew and Luke as containing myths and legends rather than history. But as I cannot consider the life and character and influence of Jesus without having forced upon me the conclusion that He was more than a man, that He was indeed God manifest in the flesh, these accounts of a supernatural birth seem altogether credible to me. In other words, If I were to cease to regard Jesus Christ as a divine being I might easily cease to believe in the virgin birth. . . . But surely there is nothing incredible in the notion that a supernatural being should have come into the world in a supernatural manner."

"I hold, therefore, that the question of the virgin birth is inextricably bound up with the question of Christ's divinity.

The Virgin Birth

If, then, one should say to me, I do not believe in the virgin birth, I would straightway ask him, Do you believe in the divinity of Jesus? If he answered No, and could not be moved from that position, I would cherish little hope of being able to persuade him that a virgin was the mother of Jesus. But if he answered Yes, then I would cherish such a hope because I should feel that a mere acquaintance with the facts of the case would be sufficient to convince him of this truth. That I am warranted in this is evidenced by the fact that practically all of those who reject the divinity of Jesus reject at the same time the virgin birth, while practically all of those who accept the divinity of Jesus accept at the same time the virgin birth. . . . The question of the virgin birth is but part of the larger question of Christ's divinity, or, to speak strictly, of His Deity. Do we on Christmas Day merely commemorate the birth of a great man? Then the accounts of Matthew and Luke may well seem incredible. Do we on that day commemorate the coming into this world of the only begotten Son of God? Then there is nothing incredible in the Gospel accounts, because everything is in perfect harmony with what might be expected at the coming of such a being into this world."[3]

We have already pointed out that when Christ became incarnate He took into union with Himself not another human person but impersonal human nature, and that for two different reasons: first, to have taken another person into union with Himself would have given Him a double personality; and secondly, union with another person would have involved Him in original sin; for all of Adam's sons have his sin imputed to them. We have also pointed out that guilt and depravity are attached not to human nature as such, but to

---
3. *Jesus As He Was and Is*, p. 50.

individual persons, specifically to all those for whom Adam stood in the covenant of works. Since Christ already possessed personality in His divine nature, He needed only to add to Himself impersonal human nature in order that He might enter into all of the experiences which are common to men. By adding human nature He became organically a part of the human race, as truly man as He was God, and therefore capable of acting as man's representative before the throne of God. Furthermore, we should keep in mind the fact that at the beginning of the race the covenant of works was made not with Eve but with Adam, and that it was Adam who was appointed the federal head and representative of the race. Through his fall every one of his descendants became involved in his guilt and pollution, that is, in original sin, which is judicially imputed to them. While Eve also fell, she occupied no such official position as did Adam; and it seems at least plausible to believe that original sin would not, indeed, could not have been charged to her descendants except as they were also sons of Adam. The consequences of disobedience were inherited only from Adam, who was the father of the race. But the Scriptures, from which we derive all our knowledge concerning our covenant relationship both with Adam and with Christ, tell us that Christ was born of the Virgin Mary, God alone being His Father. Hence while He inherited human nature from His mother, He did not inherit a personality and was therefore not chargeable with Adam's sin. Hence the vital importance of the doctrine of the virgin birth, indicating not only the supernatural character of the person so born, but also His absolute separateness from the sin of Adam.

Concerning this subject Dr. Wm. C. Robison has said: "As our Lord's divine nature had no mother, so His human nature has no father. The Son of man is no man's son. The virgin birth has guided the Church in her efforts to understand and state the union of God and man, and this break in the ordinary generations descending from Adam has presented One unstained by original sin to be the sinner's substitute. The virgin birth is integral to the virgin life and the vicarious death, to the full truthfulness of the Gospels, and to the Church's faith in the incarnation of the pre-existing Lord."[4]

And Dr. Warfield says: "It is only in its relation to the New Testament doctrine of redemption that the necessity of the virgin birth of Jesus comes to its full manifestation. For in this Christianity the redemption that is provided is distinctly redemption from sin; and that He might redeem men from sin it certainly was imperative that the Redeemer Himself should not be involved in sin. . . . Assuredly no one, himself under the curse of sin, could atone for the sin of others; no one owing the law its extreme penalty for himself could pay this penalty for others. And certainly in the Christianity of the New Testament every natural member of the race of Adam rests under the curse of Adam's sin, and is held under the penalty that hangs over it. If the Son of God came into the world therefore—as that Christianity asserts to be a 'faithful saying'—specifically in order to save sinners, it was imperatively necessary that He should become incarnate after a fashion which would leave Him standing, so far as His own responsibility is concerned, outside that fatal entail of sin in which the whole natural race of Adam is involved. And that is as much as to say that

---

4. Article in the *Moody Monthly*.

the redemptive work of the Son of God depends upon His supernatural birth."[5]

The doctrine of the Virgin Birth thus emerges as an essential doctrine of the Christian system, not in the sense that it is impossible for one to be saved unless he has a clear knowledge and firm conviction of it, but in the sense that no statement of the Christian system which ignores or denies it can be considered consistent or complete.

---
5. *Christology and Criticism*, p. 455.

XIX.

CHRIST THE MESSIAH OF OLD TESTAMENT PROPHECY

IT IS generally recognized that revelation concerning all of the great doctrines of the Bible has been progessive, that what was only vaguely intimated at first is set forth clearly and fully as time goes on. This we find to be particularly true in regard to the person and work of the Messiah. In the very nature of the case men could have no adequate comprehension of His person and work until He actually came and lived among them; and yet since the whole system of redemption was so vitally and necessarily tied up with Him it is only reasonable to suspect that some foregleams and intimations would have been given in Old Testament times. And that is exactly what we do find. In the providence of God this wonderful personality of the Messiah was not flashed before our eyes like the sun rising at midnight to dazzle and blind us, but was revealed gradually, precept upon precept, line upon line, here a little, there a little, until our understanding was prepared to receive the whole truth. It is our purpose in this chapter to trace the course of that development and to show that the Old Testament revelations concerning the person and work of the Messiah led up to and had their complete fulfillment in Christ.

The first promise concerning the coming of a Messiah who was to redeem His people is found in the third chapter of Genesis. Immediately after the fall of our first parents a curse was pronounced upon Satan who had been the immediate cause of their fall, and in that curse is contained a veiled promise of redemption: "I will put enmity between thee and the woman, and between thy seed and her seed: He shall bruise thy head, and thou shalt bruise His heel," Gen. 3:15. But while this promise was deeply veiled it was a definite ray of light in the dark night of sin which had settled down over Adam and Eve, and as such it was sufficient to keep them from despair. "The meaning of this promise and prediction," says Dr. Hodge, "is to be determined by subsequent revelations. When interpreted in the light of the Scriptures themselves, it is manifest that the seed of the woman means the Redeemer, and that bruising the serpent's head means His final triumph over the powers of darkness. In this protevangelium, as it has ever been called, we have the dawning revelation of the humanity and divinity of the great deliverer. As seed of the woman His humanity is distinctly asserted, and the nature of the triumph which He was to effect, in the subjugation of Satan, proves that He was to be a divine person. In the great conflict between the kingdom of light and the kingdom of darkness, between Christ and Belial, between God and Satan, He that triumphs over Satan, is, and can be nothing less than divine. In the earliest books of Scripture, even in Genesis, we have therefore clear intimations of the two great truths; first, that there is a plurality of persons in the Godhead; and secondly, that one of those persons is specially concerned in the salvation of men,—in their guidance, government, instruction, and ultimate deliverance from all the evils of their apostasy."[1]

We may add further concerning this promise found in Genesis 3:15 that within it is inferred both the completeness of Christ's victory and also something of the great cost at which that victory would be secured, in that to bruise or

---

1. *Systematic Theology*, I, 484.

crush the head is to inflict a fatal wound, while the bruised heel, though very painful, is not fatal.

It is quite possible that Adam and Eve, like the people of every later generation, looked for or at least hoped for the fulfillment of that promise within their lifetime. When their first son Cain was born Eve said, "I have gotten a man with the help of Jehovah," Gen. 4:1; and when Cain turned out bad and a later son in which they had great hope was born Eve called his name Seth, "For, said she, God hath appointed me another seed instead of Abel," Gen. 4:25. Generations later when Noah was born this same hope seems to have been in evidence, for we read that his father gave him this name (which means "rest"), saying, "This same shall comfort us in our work and in the toil of our hands, which cometh because of the ground which Jehovah hath cursed," Gen. 5:29. Likewise it is quite possible that some of the promises made to David concerning the greatness of his Son who was to sit on his throne, which promises had a preliminary and partial fulfillment in Solomon, led some to believe that the appearance of the Redeemer was near.

In Gen. 22:18 is recorded the promise given to Abraham: "In thy seed shall all the nations of the earth be blessed." To quote Dr. Hodge again, "He who was promised to Adam as the seed of the woman, it was next declared should be of the seed of Abraham. That this does not refer to his descendants collectively, but to Christ individually, we know from the direct assertion of the Apostle (Gal. 3:16), and from the direct fulfillment of the promise. It is not through the children of Abraham as a nation, but through Christ, that all the nations of the earth are blessed. And the blessing referred to, the promise to Abraham, which, as the Apostle says, has come upon us, is the promise of redemption. Abraham therefore saw the day of Christ and was glad, and as our Lord said, Before Abraham was I am. This proves that the person predicted as the son of the woman and as the seed of Abraham, through whom redemption was to be effected, was to be both God and man. He could not be the seed of Abraham unless man, and he could not be the Saviour of men unless God."[2]

In Gen. 49:10 the dying Jacob, speaking by inspiration and foretelling what would happen to the different tribes in the latter days, says concerning Judah:

"*The sceptre shall not depart from Judah,
Nor the ruler's staff from between his feet,
Until Shiloh come;
And unto Him shall the obedience of the people be,*"

— and while the meaning here is not altogether clear, it is generally understood to mean that Judah was to continue as a nation with at least a nominal king until the coming of the Messiah (which as a matter of historical record is what did happen, the Jews being finally dispersed shortly after that); from which time the Lord's people were to know their Messiah personally, to acknowledge Him as their true and rightful King, and so to give their allegiance to Him.

The prophet Balaam, when besought by Balak, king of Moab, to pronounce a curse on the Israelites pronounced instead a blessing, which, while having its preliminary fulfillment in David, evidently can have its complete fulfillment only in Christ:

"*There shall come forth a star out of Jacob,
And a sceptre shall rise out of Israel,
And shall smite through the corners of Moab,
And break down all the sons of tumult.*" Nu. 24:17.

In Deut. 18:18, 19 we find a remarkable prophecy given through Moses: "I will raise them up a prophet from among

---

[2]. *Systematic Theology*, I, 485.

Christ the Messiah of Old Testament Prophecy 141

their brethren, like unto thee; and I will put my words in His mouth, and He shall speak unto them all that I shall command Him. And it shall come to pass, that whosoever will not hearken unto my words which He shall speak in my name, I will require it of him." Concerning this prophecy ex-Rabbi Leopold Cohn says: "Every Jewish scholar will admit that there has not been any other prophet like unto Moses outside of the Lord Jesus, who was even greater than Moses. That this promised future prophet is identical with the Angel of Exodus 23:21 is proved by God's command to obey Him. In addition to all these previous names and characteristics God calls Him here prophet and tells us that He will be born of a woman and be like one of our brethren. And notice, please, the particular punishment for disobeying this wonderful person. 'I will require it of him.' That means that in case of Israel's disobedience to the Messiah, God is going to punish continually until they repent and obey."

In II Samuel 7:12-16 we find a great promise made to King David: "When thy days are fulfilled, and thou shalt sleep with thy fathers, I will set up thy seed after thee, that shall proceed out of thy bowels, and I will establish his kingdom. . . . I will be his father, and he shall be my son. . . . my loving kindness shall not depart from him. . . . And thy house and thy kingdom shall be made sure for ever before thee: thy throne shall be established for ever." In Ps. 89:3, 4, 36 the same promise is repeated:

"I have made a covenant with my chosen,
I have sworn unto David my servant:
Thy seed will I establish for ever,
And build up thy throne to all generations . . .
His seed shall endure for ever,
And his throne as the sun before me."

This promise receives a preliminary fulfillment in David's son Solomon, but in the very nature of the case could not be completely fulfilled in him. Its real fulfillment, as we learn from the New Testament, was reserved for the Messiah, of whom it is said that He was "the son of David," Matt. 1:1; that "He shall be great, and shall be called the Son of the Most High: and the Lord God shall give unto Him the throne of His father David: and He shall reign over the house of Jacob for ever; and of His kingdom there shall be no end," Luke 1:32,33. In Heb. 1:5 the writer specifically applies to Christ the words of the promise spoken to David in II Sam. 7:14:

"*I will be to Him a Father,
And He shall be to me a Son;*"

as also in Heb. 1:8 he applies to Christ the words of the Messianic 45th Psalm (vs. 6):

"*Thy throne, O God, is for ever and ever;
And the sceptre of uprightness is the sceptre of thy kingdom.*"

In the Messianic psalms the coming King is set forth as One who is Deity. In the 110th we read,

"*Jehovah saith unto my Lord, Sit thou at my right hand,
Until I make thine enemies thy footstool,*"

—words of one Jehovah spoken to another (and understandable only in the light of the doctrine of the Trinity), in which David, speaking by inspiration of the Holy Spirit, acknowledges that his greater Son shall be his Lord, words which Christ declared found their fulfillment in Himself (Matt. 22:21-44). In the 96th Psalm the coming of Jehovah to establish a reign of righteousness in all the earth is exultantly announced:

"*Let the heavens be glad, and let the earth rejoice;
Let the sea roar, and the fulness thereof;
Let the field exult, and all that is therein;*

*Then shall all the trees of the wood sing for joy
Before Jehovah; for He cometh,
For He cometh to judge the earth:
He will judge the world with righteousness,
And the peoples with His truth,"* vss. 11-13.
*"I will tell of the decree:
Jehovah said unto me, Thou art my Son;
This day have I begotten thee.
Ask of me, and I will give thee the nations for thine inheritance,
And the uttermost parts of the earth for thy possession,"*

Ps. 2:7,8,—quoted by the writer of the Epistle to the Hebrews (1:5) as having been spoken of Christ.

*"Thy throne, O God, is for ever and ever:
A sceptre of equity is the sceptre of thy kingdom,"*

Ps. 45:6,—declared in Heb. 1:8 to have been fulfilled in Christ.

The book of Isaiah contains a wealth of material descriptive of the Messiah. In chapter 6 Isaiah records the glorious vision in which he saw Jehovah sitting upon a throne high and lifted up and surrounded by the hosts of adoring angels who worship Him; and in the New Testament the Apostle John, after quoting the words which were spoken to Isaiah at the time of this vision and comparing the unbelief of the people in Christ to that which prevailed in Isaiah's day, declared that the person who was seen by Isaiah was none other than Christ: "These things said Isaiah, because he saw His glory; and he spake of Him," John 12:41. The divinely appointed sign by which the Messiah was to be recognized was that He should be born of a virgin: "Therefore the Lord Himself will give you a sign: behold, a virgin shall conceive, and bear a son, and shall call His name Immanuel," Is. 7:14 —than which a name more expressive of His Deity could not have been given; and Matthew, after declaring that this prophecy had its fulfillment in the virgin birth of Christ, adds that the name Immanuel, "being interpreted," means "God with us," i.e., God in our nature (1:23).

In Is. 9:2 the prophet says concerning the inhabitants of Zebulun and Naphtali: "The people that walked in darkness have seen a great light: they that dwelt in the land of the shadow of death, upon them hath the light shined;" and Matthew declares that these words were fulfilled when Christ came and dwelt in the city of Capernaum (4:13-16).

In Is. 9:6,7 we have a very remarkable and impressive description of the Messiah: "For unto us a child is born, unto us a Son is given; and the government shall be upon His shoulder: and His name shall be called Wonderful Counsellor, Mighty God, Everlasting Father, Prince of Peace. Of the increase of His government and of peace there shall be no end, upon the throne of David, and upon His kingdom, to establish it, and to uphold it with justice and with righteousness from henceforth even for ever." Here both His humanity and His Deity are clearly foretold, and it is declared that His kingdom, which is to be founded on justice and righteousness, shall be everlasting and universal. Here the term "Mighty God" is applied directly to the Messiah; and the fact that this same term is used again in chapter 10:21 where it means Jehovah shows clearly that the Messiah is declared to be God in the very same sense in which Jehovah is God. To apply those great titles to a merely human representative of Jehovah would involve the Old Testament revelation in self-contradiction; and by no manner of treatment, however ingenious, could that self-contradiction be resolved, without doing violence to all linguistic propriety. It is resolved, however, by the New Testament miracle of the Incarnation of the Son of God, so that the Messiah is at one and the same time Divine and human, the God-man. That this prophecy relates

Christ the Messiah of Old Testament Prophecy 145

to the Messiah was not disputed even by the Jews until the violence and bitterness of the anti-Christian controversy drove them from the ground which their own progenitors had steadfastly maintained.

In Is. 11:1-10 we have another description in figurative language of the reign of the Messiah as the King of the Golden Age, in which righteousness and peace are to be triumphant over all the earth and forces which have been perpetually at enmity with each other are to be reconciled in Him: "There shall come forth a shoot out of the stock of Jesse, and a branch out of his roots shall bear fruit. And the Spirit of Jehovah shall rest upon Him, and the spirit of wisdom and understanding, the spirit of counsel and might, the spirit of knowledge and of the fear of Jehovah. And His delight shall be in the fear of Jehovah; and He shall not judge after the sight of His eyes, neither decide after the hearing of His ears; but with righteousness shall he judge the poor, and decide with equity for the meek of the earth: and He shall smite the earth with the rod of His mouth; and with the breath of His lips shall He slay the wicked. And righteousness shall be the girdle of His waist, and faithfulness the girdle of His loins.

"And the wolf shall dwell with the lamb, and the leopard shall lie down with the kid; and the calf and the young lion and the fatling together; and a little child shall lead them. And the cow and the bear shall feed; their young ones shall lie down together; and the lion shall eat straw like the ox. And the suckling child shall play on the hole of the asp, and the weaned child shall put his hand on the adder's den. They shall not hurt nor destroy in all my holy mountain; for the earth shall be full of the knowledge of Jehovah, as the waters cover the sea.

"And it shall come to pass in that day, that the root of

Jesse, that standeth for an ensign of the peoples, unto Him shall the nations seek; and His resting-place shall be glorious."

Note the striking parallel between Isaiah's description of the Messiah's complete conquest over the forces of evil when he says, "He shall smite the earth with the rod of His mouth; and with the breath of the lips shall He slay the wicked" (11:4), and the description of Christ's complete conquest of the world by the preached word of the Gospel as given by John in the book of Revelation: "And out of His mouth proceedeth a sharp sword, that with it He should smite the nations: and He shall rule them with a rod of iron" (19:15). Surely no one can deny that Isaiah and John were describing the same person.

In Is. 35:5-10 the very signs and miracles which were to mark the advent of the Messiah were foretold: "Then the eyes of the blind shall be opened, and the ears of the deaf shall be unstopped. Then shall the lame man leap as a hart, and the tongue of the dumb shall sing. . . ." And when the disciples of John the Baptist came to Jesus and asked if He were the Messiah or if they should look for another, it was to these very miracles that He pointed as proof that He was the Messiah: "Go and tell John the things which ye hear and see: the blind receive their sight, and the lame walk, the lepers are cleansed, and the deaf hear, and the dead are raised up, and the poor have good tidings preached unto them," Matt. 11:4,5.

In Is. 42:1-7 the prophet again speaks of the coming age of justice and righteousness, with special mention of blessing to the Gentiles which is a distinctive characteristic of the Gospel age. To the same effect he says in 49:6: "I will give thee for a light to the Gentiles, that thou mayest be my salvation unto the end of the earth." And in the New Testament Luke tells us that when the infant Jesus was presented in the temple the aged and saintly Simeon was given to see that this was the long expected Messiah, and that he praised God with these words:

"Now lettest thou thy servant depart, Lord,
According to thy word in peace;
For mine eyes have seen thy salvation,
Which thou hast prepared before the face of all peoples;
A light for revelation to the Gentiles,
And the glory of thy people Israel" (9:29-32).

Paul calls special attention to this promise that the blessings of the Gospel are to be extended unto the uttermost parts of the Gentile world, Acts 13:47, as does also the Apostle James, Acts 15:17.

The most familiar and the most complete of all the Messianic prophecies is, of course, that found in the 53rd chapter of Isaiah (with which also belongs Is. 52:13-15). Here the nature of His work as suffering, together with its purely vicarious or substitutionary character, is clearly set forth as the only ground on which the sins of His people are forgiven:

"Who hath believed our message? and to whom hath the arm of Jehovah been revealed? For He grew up before Him as a tender plant, and as a root out of a dry ground: He hath no form nor comeliness; and when we see Him, there is no beauty that we should desire Him. He was despised, and rejected of men; a man of sorrows, and acquainted with grief: and as one from whom men hide their face he was despised; and we esteemed Him not.

"Surely He hath borne our griefs, and carried our sorrows; yet we did esteem Him stricken, smitten of God, and afflicted. But He was wounded for our transgressions, He was bruised for our iniquities; the chastisement of our peace was upon Him; and with His stripes we are healed. All we like sheep have gone astray; ye have turned every one to his own way; and Jehovah hath laid on Him the iniquity of us all.

"He was oppressed, yet when He was afflicted He opened not His mouth; as a lamb that is led to the slaughter, and as a sheep that before its shearers is dumb, so He openeth not His mouth. By oppression and judgment He was taken away; and as for His generation, who among them considered that He was cut off out of the land of the living for the transgression of my people to whom the stroke was due? And they made His grave with the wicked, and with a rich man in His death; although He had done no violence, neither was any deceit in His mouth.

"Yet it pleased Jehovah to bruise Him; He hath put Him to grief: when thou shalt make His soul an offering for sin, He shall see His seed, He shall prolong His days, and the pleasure of Jehovah shall prosper in His hand. He shall see of the travail of His soul, and shall be satisfied; by the knowledge of Himself shall my righteous servant justify many; and He shall bear their iniquities. Therefore will I divide Him a portion with the great, and He shall divide the spoil with the strong; because He poured out His soul unto death, and was numbered with the transgressors."

Isaiah 65:17-25 and 66:22, 23 portray the glorious kingdom which eventually is to result from the Messiah's work, as the Gospel is preached to ever larger numbers of men and the world is effectively turned to righteousness. The Lord's people are to be redeemed not only from the Babylonian captivity, but from all evil; and not merely the Jews but the Gentiles as well are to share in these blessings,—when "the residue of men," and "all the Gentiles," are to "seek after the Lord," Amos 9:11, 12; Acts 15:17. For Jehovah is no

Christ the Messiah of Old Testament Prophecy   149

mere tribal deity, but "the God of the whole earth." Up to the present time we have had only a foretaste of this great Golden Age, and that in very limited communities. But we see the forces of righteousness advancing, and the forces of evil in retreat; and we look forward to the time when the Gospel shall have won its complete victory and when (as a result of man's increased diligence and his advanced knowledge in the realms of agriculture, biology, chemistry, engineering, etc.) even nature shall reflect gloriously the change that has occured in the hearts of men,—"when the wilderness and the dry land shall be glad; and the desert shall rejoice and blossom as the rose," Is. 35:1.

In Jer. 23:5,6 we have another Messianic prophecy: "Behold, the days come, saith Jehovah, that I will raise unto David a righteous Branch, and He shall reign as King and deal wisely, and shall execute justice and righteousness in the land. In His days Judah shall be saved, and Israel shall deal safely; and this is His name whereby He shall be called: Jehovah our righteousness." In these verses we are told that the restoration of God's people is to be accomplished by One who is, (1) a descendant of David; (2) who is to be a king; (3) whose kingdom is to be founded, not on political or military power, but on wisdom, justice and righteousness; (4) who is called the "Branch," a term which in the book of Isaiah is applied to the Messiah; (5) His reign shall bring peace and harmony,—Judah and Israel, *i.e.*, the Lord's people, are to be united; and (6) He is expressly called "Jehovah our righteousness" (the New Testament makes it clear that we are saved not by any righteousness of our own but only by the righteousness of Christ imputed to us and received by faith alone). Consequently the name identifies Him as Christ, the Messiah. And the parallel passage of Jer. 33:14-18 declares that the kingship and the priesthood are to be permanently established through the work of this righteous Branch.

In Dan. 2:44 the kingdom of the Messiah (which was to be preceded by four great world kingdoms, the last of which was the Roman) was foretold as everlasting and as designed to supercede and absorb all other kingdoms: "And in the days of those kings shall the God of heaven set up a kingdom which shall never be destroyed, nor shall the sovereignty thereof be left to another people; but it shall break in pieces and consume all those kingdoms, and it shall stand for ever." Nearly two thousand years have elapsed since the Christian kingdom was set up by the advent of Christ in Palestine. It is still far from its consummation, but it is making progress and its triumph is certain. Already its influence is felt in almost every part of the world. To us who live in the twentieth century, as to the Christians who have lived in each preceding century, it is given to witness a small part of this mighty struggle, this battle of Armageddon, as the forces of good and evil are locked in a titanic battle for the mastery of the world,—while indeed "the kingdom of the world" is slowly but surely becoming "the kingdom of our Lord, and of His Christ," Rev. 11:15.

In the vision recorded in Dan. 7:13,14 we witness a veritable coronation act which, in the light of the New Testament, we recognize as the reward conferred upon Christ for His work of redemption: "I saw in the night-visions, and, behold, there came with the clouds of heaven one like unto a Son of Man, and He came even to the Ancient of Days, and they brought Him near before Him. And there was given Him dominion, and glory, and a kingdom, that all the peoples, nations, and languages should serve Him: His dominion is an everlasting dominion which shall not pass away, and His kingdom that which shall not be destroyed." Here the

Christ the Messiah of Old Testament Prophecy 151

transcendental element of the Messianic figure, the "Son of Man," is so strongly stressed that the human traits are almost obscured. Here He is represented as coming with the clouds, which symbolize divine majesty,—a description which is never applied to any other than the Lord of nature, for He alone can ride on the clouds of heaven. It was from this description that Jesus derived His favorite title, "Son of Man," in the use of which He presented Himself as a heavenly Being come to earth on a mission of mercy to lost men. At the trial of Jesus before the Sanhedrin it was His use of this title together with its appropriate setting from Dan. 7:13,14 which so infuriated the high priest that he rent his garments and declared that Jesus had spoken blasphemy (Matt. 26:64).

In Micah 5:2-5 is found the well-known prediction that the Messiah was to be born in Bethlehem: "But thou, Bethlehem Ephrathah, which art little to be among the thousands of Judah, out of thee shall come forth unto me that is to be ruler in Israel; whose goings forth are from of old, from everlasting. . . . And He shall stand, and shall feed His flock in the strength of Jehovah, in the majesty of the name of Jehovah His God: and they shall abide; for now shall He be great unto the ends of the earth. And this man shall be our peace." Concerning these verses Dr. Hodge says: "The prophet Micah predicted that one was to be born in Bethlehem, who was to be, (1) The Ruler of Israel, *i.e.*, of all the people of God. (2) Although to be born in time and made of a woman, His 'goings forth are from of old, from everlasting.' (3) He shall rule in the exercise of the strength and majesty of God, *i.e.*, manifest in His government the possession of divine attributes and glory. (4) His dominion shall be universal; and (5) Its effects peace, *i.e.*, perfect harmony, order, blessedness."[1] And that these verses were understood by the Jews to predict the advent of the Messiah is proved from Matt. 2:4-6, where, in response to Herod's inquiry as to where the Christ should be born, the priests and scribes readily replied by quoting Micah 5:2.

In Zechariah the Messiah is described as the "King," who is "just, and having salvation; lowly, and riding upon an ass, even upon a colt the foal of an ass," 9:9 (with which compare Matthew's account of Jesus' public entry into Jerusalem, 21:1-11); whose dominion is to be universal: "His dominion shall be from sea to sea, and from the River unto the ends of the earth," 9:10; who is to be sold for thirty pieces of silver, 11:12,13 (with which compare Matthew's account of Judas' treachery, 26:14-16). Because the Jews rejected the Messiah they have brought upon themselves untold suffering and reproach and have been given up to long dispersion. This too was foretold by Zechariah: "I will scatter them with a whirlwind among all the nations which they have not known," 7:14,—and this is precisely what they have experienced during these nineteen centuries that have elapsed since that time. But happily Zechariah tells us something more. At long last God is to pour out upon the people of Israel "the spirit of grace and of supplication," and they are to turn to the Messiah and repent: "And they shall mourn for Him, as one mourneth for his only son, and shall be in bitterness for Him, as one that is in bitterness for his first-born," 12:10. When Christ was on earth they hid, as it were, their faces from Him; but now they are to look to Him in true penitence, and they are to mourn with a peculiarly bitter sorrow. Furthermore, His kingdom is to triumph and become universal: "Jehovah shall be King over all the earth,"

---
1. *Systematic Theology*, I, 493.

Christ the Messiah of Old Testament Prophecy 153

14:9; wealth is to be greatly increased (14:4), and holiness is to prevail everywhere (14:11,16,20,21).

And Malachi, the last of the Old Testament prophets, declares that "The Lord, whom ye seek, will suddenly come to His temple; and the Messenger of the covenant, whom ye desire, behold, He cometh, saith Jehovah of hosts," 3:1; and again, "Unto you that fear my name shall the Sun of Righteousness arise with healing in its wings," 4:2. Like the other prophets, he too foretells a reign of righteousness and peace, emphasizing that the Gentiles as well as the Jews are to share its blessings: "For from the rising of the sun even unto the going down of the same my name shall be great among the Gentiles; and in every place incense shall be offered unto my name, and a pure offering: for my name shall be great among the Gentiles, saith Jehovah of hosts," 1:11 (also 3:2-5, 11, 12; 4:3). And at the very close of his book and of the Old Testament, as if it were a sign post pointing across the silent centuries to the New Testament, we find the prophecy that Elijah the prophet is to return and prepare the way for the Messiah (4:5, 6),—which prophecy, Matthew tells us, was fulfilled in John the Baptist, who came in the spirit and power of Elijah and prepared the way for Jesus (11:10; 17:10-13).

Thus we find that from the very first the Old Testament clearly and repeatedly predicts the advent of a divine person clothed in our nature, who was to be the Redeemer of His people. As the revelation is unfolded by the procession of the prophets He is set forth as truly man, the seed of the woman, the seed of Abraham, of the tribe of Judah, a prophet like unto Moses, of the house of David, a man of sorrows and acquainted with grief, to be born of a virgin, in the village of Bethlehem; He is to be lowly in manner, He is to be heralded by one reminiscent of the prophet Elijah, and

He is suddenly to come to His Temple. Yet it was no less clearly revealed that He was to be a divine person, the Mighty God, One who would exercise divine prerogatives and receive divine worship from men and angels, One who would accredit Himself before the people by working miracles of healing on the blind, the lame, the deaf and the dumb, a triumphant King whose dominion is to be extended until it embraces the entire world. Sometimes the Divine, sometimes the human side of His nature is held up more prominently by the prophets. And, as the New Testament makes clear, these prophecies were literally fulfilled in Christ. The specific purpose for which they were given was to make it possible for the people to recognize the Messiah at once by comparing these descriptions with His person and work. But alas, that those to whom the Scriptures were entrusted were so blind that they not only failed to recognize Him, but even rejected Him with the most abusive and shameful treatment!

Thus the outstanding element in the eschatological system of the Old Testament was the expectation that in some majestic way God would again come to His people and walk and talk with them as He had done in the Garden of Eden. From the very beginning the Jewish religion was a religion of hope, and also from the very beginning it was prepared sometime to become the world-religion. Far from the Messianic idea being merely the expectation of an outstanding earthly king and having been developed late in the history of Israel as some of the critics would have us believe, the devout-minded in Israel had ever before them the hope that their salvation would be made sure through the appearance of Jehovah in person. Throughout the Old Testament period they looked for salvation to the same Christ that we look to, and never were they encouraged to look to any other.

Christ the Messiah of Old Testament Prophecy 155

The New Testament takes up the narrative concerning the Messiah at just the point where the Old Testament had left off. Everywhere the Christ of the New Testament is presented as the One who fulfills the Messianic prophecies of the Old. Matthew begins his Gospel by tracing the genealogy of Jesus through David and Abraham. He records the virgin birth of Jesus as the fulfillment of the prophecy in Is. 7:14, His birth in Bethlehem as the fulfillment of Micah 5:2, and the ministry of John the Baptist as the fulfillment of Is. 40:3. Mark begins his Gospel by declaring that Jesus Christ is the Son of God, and that the ministry of John the Baptist fulfills the prophecies in Is. 40:3 and Mal. 3:1. Luke, in recording the words of the angel Gabriel, says concerning Jesus that "He shall be great, and shall be called the Son of the Most High: and the Lord God shall give unto Him the throne of His father David: and He shall reign over the house of Jacob for ever; and of His kingdom there shall be no end," 1:32, 33. He also records the testimony of the aged and saintly Simeon who, when Jesus was presented in the temple, recognized Him as the Messiah through whom God would provide salvation, and as "A light for revelation to the Gentiles, And the glory of thy people Israel," 2:32. John begins his Gospel with a Prologue in which he sets forth the Deity of the incarnate "Word," and relates Jesus intimately to the Old Testament doctrine of redemption with the designation, "The Lamb of God, that taketh away the sin of the world," 1:29.

There is, of course, no doubt but that Jesus Himself claimed to be the Messiah. Early in His ministry, in response to the words of the woman of Samaria, "I know that Messiah cometh," He said: "I that speak unto thee am He," John 4:26. He accepted as accurate and as His just due the words of Peter, "Thou art the Christ, the Son of the living God," Matt.

16:16, and declared that this truth had been revealed to him not by men but by His Father who is in heaven. He accepted also the testimony of Martha: "I have believed that thou art the Christ, the Son of God, even He that cometh into the world," John 11:27. To the Pharisees He said, "Except ye believe that I am He, ye shall die in your sins," John 8:24,—than which a more stupendous claim could hardly be made. In His controversy with the Pharisees He pointed out that their ideas of the Messiah fell far below the teaching of their own Scriptures; for while they thought of Him only as David's son, the Scriptures presented Him also as David's Lord (Matt. 22:41-45). When the disciples of John the Baptist came to ask if He were the Messiah, or if they should look for another, He replied, "Go and tell John the things which ye hear and see: the blind receive their sight, and the lame walk, the lepers are cleansed, and the deaf hear, and the dead are raised up, and the poor have good tidings preached to them," Matt. 11:4, 5. These and similar miracles were the very signs that Isaiah had said would accompany the work of the Messiah (35:5, 6). In response to the request of the Jews that if He were the Christ He tell them plainly, Jesus said, "I told you, and ye believe not: the works that I do in my Father's name, these bear witness of me," John 10:25. These miracles should have been sufficient evidence to have convinced any one. Such evidence was sufficient for the woman at the well in Samaria who, free from prejudice and acting only on her simple faith and common sense and with characteristic reticence, said to the people of the town, "Come, see a man, who told me all things that ever I did: can this be the Christ?" John 4:29. They were sufficient to convince the disciples (John 2:11; Luke 5:8), as well as many of the common people (John 6:14; 10:42; 11:45; 12:11). Jesus' public entry into Jerusalem at

Christ the Messiah of Old Testament Prophecy 157

the beginning of passion week was especially designed to manifest publicly His claims to Messiahship (Luke 19:29-40). And during the trial before the Sanhedrin He claimed under oath and in a most public and explicit manner that He was the Messiah. In response to the charge of the high priest, "I adjure thee by the living God, that thou tell us whether thou art the Christ, the Son of the living God," Jesus answered, "Thou hast said: nevertheless I say unto you, Henceforth ye shall see the Son of Man sitting at the right hand of Power, and coming on the clouds of heaven," Matt. 26:64.

As Jesus met with the disciples after the resurrection He completed the revelation that He had been making concerning Himself, pointing out to them how the Old Testament had predicted His sufferings and the glory that was to follow. In Luke 24:25-27 we are told that Jesus, as He walked with the disciples on the road to Emmaus, rebuked them for not perceiving the clear teaching of the Old Testament concerning His sufferings: "O foolish men, and slow of heart to believe in all that the prophets have spoken! Behooved it not the Christ to suffer these things, and to enter into His glory? And beginning from Moses and from all the prophets, He interpreted to them in all the Scriptures the things concerning Himself." No doubt He brought out the meaning of many other texts which we have not yet understood. Earlier He had said to the Jews, "If ye believed Moses, ye would have believed me; for he wrote of me," John 5:46. Even before His incarnation and suffering lighted up so many dark passages of the ancient Scriptures it should have been apparent that the Messiah was to be not merely a son of David according to the flesh but also Deity, and not merely a King but also One who was to bear a burden of suffering. And since the sacrificial system with its emphasis on the pascal lamb pervaded the entire religious life of the Jewish people and prefigured the atonement which was to be worked out by the Messiah, this in itself should have given a strong lead as to what the mission of the Messiah would be when He came. Hence it is clear that the Old Testament did set forth the person and work of the Messiah who was to come. Had the Jewish people been spiritually awake they would have had no difficulty at all in recognizing the Messiah.

We should also point out that the testimony of the disciples to the Messiahship of Jesus is equally strong. The Gospels are, of course, distinctly not biographies of Jesus in the sense in which we usually think of biographies. Rather they are theses written to prove that He was the promised Messiah. John in particular states the purpose of his book when he says: "Many other signs therefore did Jesus in the presence of the disciples, which are not written in this book: but these are written, that ye may believe that Jesus is the Christ, the Son of God; and that believing ye may have life in His name," 20:30, 31. Each of the Gospels is composed primarily of recorded incidents or teachings which are designed to prove the Deity or Messiahship of Christ, and the details concerning His life are brought in only incidentally. This method, however, most effectively reveals the background and brings the attributes of the supernatural Being into view in the most natural way; and the practical purpose of the writers, that of being spiritually helpful to their readers, is most effectively served. Peter, speaking for the disciples, the group that knew His life most intimately, said, "Thou art the Christ, the Son of the living God," Matt. 16:16; and again he said, "To Him bear all the prophets witness," Acts 10:43. And Philip's interpretation of the prophecies of Isaiah led the Ethiopian eunuch to the conclusion that Jesus was the Messiah so that he desired to be baptized in His name, Acts 8:26-40. Moreover in this connection it should

Christ the Messiah of Old Testament Prophecy 159

be kept in mind that the facts concerning the person and actions of Christ were well known to the early Christians to whom the Gospels and the Epistles were written, and that consequently nowhere is the doctrine of the person of Christ formally expounded. The writers very naturally did not feel the need of giving instructions concerning that which was already common property among the Christians, but in most cases only alluded incidentally to the elements in the doctrine of the person of Christ as they set Him forth as an example of conduct for others. Even in Phil. 2:5-9 where Paul, the most didactic of the New Testament writers, intimates more fully than anywhere else his conception of the person of Christ, his primary object is to set Him forth as an example of unselfishness. Although He existed as Deity before His incarnation, says Paul, He did not look selfishly upon His condition of equality with God, but emptied Himself, took the form of a servant and became obedient even to the death of the cross in order that others might share in His true riches and fulness.

The early Christian Church strongly pressed the claim that Christ was the Messiah who was foretold in the Old Testament. Peter pointed out that David, "foreseeing this spake of the resurrection of Christ, that neither was He left unto hades, nor did His flesh see corruption. This Jesus did God raise up," Acts 2:31, 32 (compare Ps. 16:8-11 and Acts 2:24-32). The point here made is that the resurrection is a proof that Jesus was the Messiah. Stephen gave his witness unflinchingly before the rulers of Israel, declaring that they had betrayed and killed "the Righteous One" whose coming had been foretold by the prophets, Acts 7:52. Paul affirms that "they that dwell in Jerusalem, and their rulers, because they knew Him not, nor the voices of the prophets which are read every Sabbath, fulfilled them by condemning

Him," Acts 13:27. The belief that Jesus was the Christ was, of course, the very corner stone of belief in the early Christian Church, the distinguishing mark which set it apart from continuing Judaism.

It is very evident that the Old Testament portrait of the Messiah was largely misunderstood by the Jewish people. The turbulent political life through which they were passing naturally had its effect on their religious life. For nearly six hundred years they had suffered under the tyranny of foreign invaders. Thus molded by oppression and poverty they had come to think of the Messianic kingdom in terms of political empire and material prosperity. So far as the official classes were concerned the purely religious hopes of the Old Testament had been almost forgotten, and even among the common people the idea of a spiritual kingdom had been largely displaced by that of an earthly kingdom. They longed for a restoration of the kingdom as it had been under David and Solomon, with added power and wealth. There were, however, some few righteous and devout souls, such as Joseph and Mary, Zecharias and Elizabeth, Simeon, the shepherds and the wise-men who saw the true spiritual import of the Messianic prophecies. But when Jesus explained to Nicodemus that entrance into the kingdom of God meant such a change of character and conduct that a man might truly be said to have been born anew, Nicodemus, although a trained religious thinker of the Jews, could not understand; and the disciples even after three years of intimate association with Jesus still found it hard to subordinate the political and military and economic aspects of the kingdom to the spiritual. Witness their question as He talked to them just before His ascension: "Lord, dost thou at this time restore the kingdom to Israel?" It is true, of course, that the Old Testament prophecies do foretell a great golden age of political freedom and material prosperity in connection with the Messianic kingdom; but this phase of the kingdom was subordinated to the spiritual, and in fact is largely future even in our own day.

We have also noted that one prominent element in the Messianic prophecies was the promise that the Gentiles were to share in the future blessings. While in Old Testament times God's revelation was given almost exclusively to the Jews (not that they might selfishly hoard it for themselves, but that they might be blessed by it and in turn pass it on to the Gentiles, in which task, however, they proved extremely derelect), and while even in the New Testament we are reminded that "Salvation is of the Jews," John 4:22 (in that our only Saviour, Jesus Christ, "as concerning the flesh," Rom. 9:5, was a Jew and the Bible is of Jewish origin), the old distinctions have been abolished and Jews and Gentiles now stand as equals before God. Within the Christian realm the distinction between Jew and Gentile, like the distinction between bond and free or male and female, means nothing. Paul tells us that all true Christians are "sons of God, through faith, in Christ Jesus. For as many of you as were baptized into Christ did put on Christ. There can be neither Jew nor Greek, there can be neither bond nor free, there can be no male and female; for ye are all one man in Christ Jesus," Gal. 3:26-28. In writing to the Gentile church in Ephesus Paul reminded them of their former condition, saying, "Ye, the Gentiles in the flesh . . . were at that time separate from Christ, alienated from the commonwealth of Israel, and strangers from the covenants of the promise, having no hope and without God in the world." And then he added: "But now in Christ Jesus ye that were afar off are made nigh in the blood of Christ. For He is our peace, who made both one, and brake down the middle wall of partition. . . . And

He came and preached peace to you that were afar off, and to them that were nigh: for through Him we both have our access in one Spirit unto the Father. So then ye are no more strangers and sojourners, but ye are fellow-citizens with the saints, and of the household of God, being built upon the foundation of the apostles and prophets, Jesus Christ Himself being the chief cornerstone," Eph. 2:11-20.

Furthermore, in matters pertaining to salvation the spiritual relationship is stronger than the physical. This principle was set forth by Christ Himself: "Whosoever shall do the will of my Father who is in heaven, he is my brother, and sister, and mother," Matt. 12:50. Paul sets forth Abraham as the typical example of the true believer, and declares that the believing Gentile is in a truer sense a son of Abraham than is an unbelieving Jew. "Know therefore that they that are of faith, the same are sons of Abraham," Gal. 3:7. And again, "If ye are Christ's then are ye Abraham's seed, heirs according to promise," Gal. 3:29. The fact of the matter is that Jews have no other righteousness than that which comes through faith in Christ, no standing whatever with God except as they acknowledge Christ as their Saviour; and Gentile believers possess fully this same righteousness by faith alone.

During the past two thousand years the Christian Church has been largely a Gentile Church, and the attitude of the Jews has been mainly that of opposition—due in part to a blind prejudice which has not allowed them to examine fairly and openly the evidence for Christianity, and also in part, it must be admitted, to the indifference or even persecution which professing Christians, both Protestants and Catholics, have directed against them. It should be pointed out, however, that such persecution is utterly contrary to all Christian principles and repulsive to all true Christians, that all

Christ the Messiah of Old Testament Prophecy 163

true Christians have a deep sympathy for the Jews as God's ancient people and as the race from which our Saviour came, and that such persecution as has taken place has been instigated by misguided or unchristian people who were betraying the very principles which they professed to hold.

It is a mistaken view which expects a future period in which God will single out the Jews and bless them above the Gentiles. Their primary mission as the channel through which the oracles of God were given, and as the race which was to provide the Saviour of the world, has been fulfilled, and they now stand on exactly the same footing as do the Gentiles, needing equally the righteousness of Christ for salvation and being utterly without hope apart from that righteousness. There are, however, numerous promises in Scripture that they, along with the Gentiles, are to be converted to Christianity. We have already noted the prophecy that they shall look upon Him whom they pierced, and that they are to mourn for Him as one mourns for his first-born. In the eleventh chapter of Romans Paul likens the Jews to the natural branches of the olive tree which were broken off and the Gentiles to wild branches which have been grafted in. He points out that "by their fall salvation is come unto the Gentiles, to provoke them to jealousy," and adds: "Now if their fall is the riches of the world, and their loss the riches of the Gentiles; how much more their fulness?" In contrast with that of the Gentiles, the spiritual energy and zeal with which they are capable of responding to their own religion is likened to "life from the dead." Paul says pointedly that "God is able to graft them in again," and that "a hardening in part hath befallen Israel, until the fulness of the Gentiles be come in; and so all Israel shall be saved: even as it is written, There shall come out of Zion the Deliverer; He shall turn away ungodliness from Jacob," Rom. 11:23, 25, 26.

How tragic it is that all these years the Jewish people should have rejected Him who in the highest sense is "the glory of His people Israel" But events sometimes take unexpected courses and, strange as it may seem, the second World War has produced a marked change in the attitude of the Jews toward Christ. Whereas for ages they have been governed by a blind hatred and opposition to Him, the very mention of His name being forbidden in the Ghetto and in the synagogue, the attitude of the Christian Church as it has attempted to shield them from persecution and to minister to them in the dictator-dominated countries has caused them to see Christianity in a new light. While no considerable numbers have yet acknowledged Christ as Messiah, many outstanding teachers and leaders have tried to outdo themselves in acknowledging Him as an incomparable teacher and leader. This in itself is, of course, not enough, but it is a long step in the right direction.

In concluding this phase of our study, then, we would point out that the Christ of the New Testament is the perfect fulfillment of the Old Testament Messianic prophecies. In His Divine-human person, the manner of His birth, His teaching, His miracles, the death He died, the redemption He accomplished, and the nature of the kingdom that He has established, the distinguishing marks of the Messiah are fully satisfied.

XX.

THE PERSONAL APPEARANCE OF JESUS

ONE rather surprising thing which emerges in connection with a study of the person of Christ is that no authentic records which we possess make any attempt to describe His physical features. Artists have painted their pictures and sculptors have made their statues, but the likenesses are imaginary. So far as His general appearance was concerned He undoubtedly appeared to be only a man, a perfectly normal man. There is, of course, not the slightest evidence which would lead us to believe that a halo of light surrounded His head, either in infancy or in later years. Isaiah's prophecy that "He hath no form nor comliness; and when we see Him, there is no beauty that we should desire Him" (53:2), seems to indicate that He was to be a perfectly normal man, that He was to possess no outward qualities which would set Him off from other men as such. But He was a very outstanding man. The phrase, "Son of Man," seems to indicate that He answered to the idea of perfect humanity as it was intended in the original creation. We are told that the people who heard Him in the days of His flesh remarked, "Never man so spake," John 7:46; that they "wondered at the words of grace which proceeded out of His mouth," Luke 4:22; and that His teaching, as contrasted with that of the scribes, was with "authority," Matt. 7:29. His were words of wisdom and power always, and we believe there never was another human voice so full of music and resonance and grace as was the voice of the Lord Jesus. It must have been a rare privilege to have heard Him speak to men, and an even more rare privilege to have heard Him when He spoke to God in prayer. It was after the disciples had heard Him pray that they felt in their hearts a great desire to be able to pray as He did, and they said, "Lord, teach us to pray, even as John also taught his disciples," Luke 11:1.

And where else in all humanity do we find such a marvelous union and balance of opposite traits as in the personality of Jesus? As Dr. E. Y. Mullins has said: "Where does humanity shine with such a radiance as in Him? Who among the sons of men were ever so 'meek and lowly in heart?' Did ever weary humanity feel a touch so tender? Did patience ever conquer so splendid a Kingdom? Did modesty and gentleness ever find so complete an incarnation? Or self-denial ever master a life so completely? Over against these lowly virtues note the heroic ones. 'All power has been given unto me," He said. 'Woe unto you scribes and Pharisees, hypocrites,' was His own hot blast of judgment. Speaking of Himself He said if this stone fall on a man it will grind him to powder. He alone was Lord and Master, the disciples were brethren. What mortal is it that hurls out this challenge, 'Which of you convicteth me of sin?' He it was who was filled with an ambition to rule the race and predicted His coming on the clouds of heaven surrounded by angels. The union of opposites in perfect balance appears in Jesus. Other men are fragments. He is the complete man. He is weary and asleep on the boat as any tired apostle might have been; but He stands up and with a voice of power stills a tempest. He weeps with the other broken-hearted ones at a grave; but with a divine voice calls forth the dead Lazarus. He yields to His captors as any culprit might have done; but works a miracle to restore a severed ear and rebuke the rash disciple who smote it off."[1]

---
1. *Why Is Christianity True?* p. 121.

The Personal Appearance of Jesus 167

There are those who have been led to see in Jesus only a sort of mild effeminate character who, while markedly free from evil, was decidedly lacking in strength and ruggedness of character. Unfortunately most of the artists have presented Him as a delicate man with a thin face and small hands. But the New Testament presents Him quite differently. The Jesus there presented was a carpenter who earned His living with His own hands; and a carpenter's hands have more of strength than delicacy, more muscle than fineness of shape. We do not know how He looked, except that He was a Jew and an oriental. But surely He was vigorous and masculine and strong, a man's man in every respect. He won the devotion of a select group of men friends. At Nazareth He walked boldly through the midst of a hostile mob that had gathered to hurl Him over a cliff; and in the garden of Gethsemane when voluntarily surrendering Himself He stepped from the shadows with such majestic personality that those who had come to arrest Him recoiled backward and fell to the ground. Bravely He went to a dreadful death and bore the world's sin in His own body on the cross. Certainly the Gospels give us to understand that He was strong, and that the whole bearing of His personality was impressive and commanding.

In this same connection the present writer on another occasion has said: "Too long the picture of Jesus as a weak, inoffensive, harmless soul has been allowed to go unchallenged. The New Testament certainly does not present Him as such a person. These characteristics have been inferred partly, no doubt, by the fact that in dealing with the erring and with those who were afflicted or in sorrow He was gentle and sympathetic; partly because of His admonition to 'resist not him that is evil' (Matt. 5:39, where the context makes it clear that He forbids the taking of revenge, not that He advocated nonresistance in general); and partly because of the fact that during His public ministry women were drawn with peculiar loyalty to His service and in many instances have been more active than men in the Church since that time. In regard to this latter consideration it is well to keep in mind that in the ordinary relationships between men and women it is the masculine qualities of strength, initiative and leadership, not the feminine qualities, which women most admire in men. The disciples and all others who saw and heard Jesus were strongly impressed with His courage, His fearlessness, His tireless energy, and His air of supreme self-confidence and leadership. Repeatedly the Gospel writers use the words 'power' and 'authority' in connection with Him. From the beginning of His public ministry until He was nailed to the cross He was in courageous opposition to the scribes and Pharisees, showing how they perverted the Scriptures, denouncing them as liars and hypocrites, and exposing their fraudulent practices. Single-handed and alone He stood against those organized groups which were holding His people in mental and spiritual bondage. He called His disciples not to a life of ease and comfort and safety, but to one of hardship and sacrifice and danger. He sent them out on a mission which would take them to the ends of the earth, and warned them that they would suffer many persecutions and in some instances death. Certainly no weakling could have inspired men for such service as that."

While at first it may strike us as strange that none of the New Testament writers has given any description of Jesus, not even so much as one of His physical features having been mentioned, that was undoubtedly a wise provision in the divine plan. It was designed in part, at least, to prevent idolatry. In all ages men have shown themselves very prone to make and worship idols. Witness not only the almost universal practice of idol worship among heathen, but also the strong tendency toward it among the Jews in Old Testament times, and even today in the professedly Christian Roman Catholic Church where countless images of Christ, the Virgin and the saints are given reverent adoration. We can hardly imagine to what extent this abuse would have been carried, especially among the more ignorant of the people, if they had possessed a real likeness of Christ. As in the earlier dispensation the grave of Moses was kept secret (Deut. 34:6) and thereby safely out of the reach of idolatry and special veneration, so here a wise directing providence has concealed the true likeness of Christ. "God is a Spirit," says John, "and they that worship Him must worship in spirit and truth," John 4:24.

It is of interest, however, to note that we have very definite information concerning one item of Jesus' dress. The pious Jew had God's command to wear a blue fringe on the border of his outer garment. The Hebrew and Greek words used to describe this fringe are variously translated by different scholars: fringe, hem, border, lace. But at any rate it was something blue on the edge of the garment. Blue is a heavenly color, the color of the sky, a reminder of God. It was one of the principal colors of the tabernacle; and one of the high priest's outer garments was of blue. The command concerning the blue fringe was given by Moses and is found in Nu. 15:37-40. After an object lesson of sin and punishment, the people then and throughout their generations were commanded to wear a blue fringe on their garments as a reminder of God and His commandments. Of the Scribes and Pharisees in Jesus' day it was said that they "made broad their phylacteries, and enlarged the borders of their garments," Matt. 23:5. It is the blue fringe that is referred to in Matt. 9:20, where we are told that the woman with an issue of blood "came behind Him, and touched the border of His garment"; and again in Matt. 14:36, where we are told that the men of Gennesaret brought to Him all that were sick, and that "they besought Him that they might only touch the border of His garment: and as many as touched were made whole." Jesus was a true Jew and preached to Jews. He came not to destroy but to fulfill the law. He was born under the Old Testament dispensation and scrupulously observed the ceremonial law throughout His entire earthly life. It was in fact His death on the cross which closed the Old Testament dispensation and ushered in the New. He was the real Lamb of God, and His sacrifice was the reality to which the Old Testament sacrifices looked forward and of which they were but the symbols and shadows. Undoubtedly He wore the blue fringe.

There is an old tradition—on what authority it rests we do not knew—which says that Jesus was never seen to laugh a single time, but that He was seen to weep. Whether that was true or not at least the spirit of it is good. That He did weep we are told in Scripture,—John 11:35. That He was never seen to laugh may at first seem strange to some. But for One who saw and fully understood fallen human nature, who knew that apart from divine grace every member of the race was hopelessly lost and on the way to eternal destruction, and who was conscious that the whole burden of redemption rested exclusively on His shoulders, life could be no laughing matter. We can laugh and enjoy life because our burden has been borne by another. Indeed, the world now has much of happiness and joy in it. But let us remember that that happiness and joy was purchased for us by One who suffered in our stead and who paid in His own person and in full the awful price that sin entails. Jesus could not be off guard for one moment, nor enter into the light-hearted pleasures in

The Personal Appearance of Jesus 171

which we indulge so freely. Rather His attitude toward life would seem to be reflected more accurately by such statements as that of Luke 9:51 where we read that "He steadfastly set His face to go to Jerusalem" (when He knew that crucifixion awaited Him), and that of Luke 12:50: "I have a baptism to be baptized with; and how am I straightened till it be accomplished!" This means primarily that His attitude toward life was one of extreme earnestness, but not that He was in any sense gloomy or morose. Witness His presence with His disciples at the wedding in Cana, where He turned the water into wine in order that the wedding festivities might proceed normally. The multitudes, we are told, heard Him gladly and sometimes were attracted to Him in such great numbers that it was humanly impossible for Him to minister to them. His birth was heralded by the angels as bringing "good tidings of great joy which shall be to all the people," Luke 2:10. Repeatedly He spoke of spiritual and heavenly joys, which in reality are the only permanent and abiding joys: Matt. 25:21; Luke 6:23; 15:7, 10; John 3:29; 15:11; 16:20, 22, 24; etc. From childhood to old age people in Christian lands have many joys which are unknown to those who live in non-Christian lands. Furthermore we may add that Christianity, far from being a kill-joy religion as so many would have us believe, is in reality the only true basis for happiness. The word "Gospel" literally means *good news*, the good news of what Christ has done for us. In fact, Christians are the only persons in this sinful world who have a genuine cause to be happy. For, despite whatever trials and hardships they may have (which trials, Paul says, "are not worthy to be compared with the glory which shall be revealed to us-ward," Rom. 8:18), their eternal happiness is assured and each passing day only brings them that much closer to that rich inheritance. But non-Christians, despite whatever worldly pleasures they may have, are, so long as they remain astray from God, only living in a fool's paradise, and each new day only brings them that much nearer their final destruction. Would that the world might see with unprejudiced eyes the true import of the Christian faith and that it might turn to that Saviour who alone can bring real and abiding joy to the human heart.

XXI.

THE OFFICES OF CHRIST

THE mediatorial work of Christ is most conveniently treated under three heads or offices. This does not mean that it can be divided into three separate and independent parts, for it cannot. But it does mean that in this form it can be presented more logically and systematically. These three offices, together with the nature of the work accomplished under each, are clearly stated in the Shorter Catechism. In answer to the question, "What offices doth Christ execute as our Redeemer?" (Question 23), the answer is given: "Christ, as our Redeemer, executeth the offices of a prophet, of a priest, and of a king, both in His estate of humiliation and and exaltation."

1. CHRIST AS PROPHET

In answer to the question, "How doth Christ execute the office of a prophet?" the Catechism answers: "Christ executeth the office of a prophet, in revealing to us, by His Word and Spirit, the will of God for our salvation." A prophet, as the term is used in Scripture, is one who speaks for another, specifically, one who is qualified and authorized to speak for God to men. Christ was, of course, the greatest of the prophets, the prophet *par excellence.* The Old Testament prophets, although real prophets who spoke God's word to the people, were in this regard but types of Christ who spoke not merely for God but as God. The revelation which they made was elementary and incomplete; that which He made was complete and final. They prefaced their messages with, "Thus saith the Lord," never presuming to speak in their own authority but only in that of God; but He said, "I say unto you." Concerning the pre-eminent place of Christ among the prophets the Apostle John says, "no man hath seen God at any time; the only begotten Son, who is in the bosom of the Father, He hath declared Him," 1:18; and the writer of the Epistle to the Hebrews begins his writing with these words: "God, having of old time spoken unto the fathers in the prophets by divers portions and in divers manners, hath at the end of these days spoken unto us in His Son, whom He appointed heir of all things, through whom also He made the world, who being the effulgence of His glory, and the very image of His substance, and upholding all things by the word of His power, when He had made purification for sins, sat down on the right hand of the Majesty on high," 1:1-3.

In both the Old and the New Testament Christ is called a prophet. "Jehovah thy God will raise up unto thee a prophet from the midst of thee, of thy brethren, like unto me," said Moses, Deut. 18:15; and in Acts 3:22 this prophecy is declared to have been fulfilled in Christ. Christ called Himself a prophet when He said, "A prophet is not without honor, save in his own country, and in his own house," Matt. 13:57; and again, "Nevertheless I must go on my way today and tomorrow and the day following: for it cannot be that a prophet perish out of Jerusalem," Luke 13:33. He was also recognized by the people as a prophet: "When therefore the people saw the sign which He did, they said, This is of a truth the prophet that cometh into the world," John 6:14.

Christ was, of course, not merely a prophet in the narrow sense of foretelling future events, but (and this is much more important) in the broad sense of being pre-eminently the Interpreter and Revealer of divine truth. It was through

Him that God's message of redemption in its fulness was communicated to man. The Old Testament prophets did sometimes predict future events, but such predictions were comparatively rare and were only incidental to their main work, which was that of calling men to repentance by earnest preaching of the law, and to faith through their proclamation of the coming redemption.

Because Christ drew from the fountainhead of all wisdom, He taught as one having authority, and not as the scribes. In all of His teaching there was never a note of indecision or doubt, never a tendency to reason things out or speculate, but always an air of authority and finality. He alone had original knowledge of God, and He alone knew the real condition of men's spiritual nature and the remedy for that condition.

In His office as prophet, then, Christ reveals to us the will of God for our salvation. Or, in other words, He proclaims to us the Gospel. That proclamation was indeed begun by Him in Old Testament times as He sent the Holy Spirit upon the prophets who testified beforehand of His coming and gave an elementary revelation of the way of salvation. But when we think of Christ as prophet we think primarily of the revelation that He gave after becoming man. All of His teaching during His earthly ministry is here included. But His work as prophet did not end with His earthly career. Before leaving the disciples He gave them the promise that the Holy Spirit would be sent to continue this work: "But when the Comforter is come, whom I will send unto you from the Father, even the Spirit of truth, who proceedeth from the Father, He shall bear witness of me: and ye also bear witness, because ye have been with me from the beginning," John 15:27, 27; "The Comforter, even the Holy Spirit, whom the Father will send in my name, He shall teach you all things, and bring to your remembrance all that I said unto you," John 14:26; "When He the Spirit of truth is come, He shall guide you into all the truth," John 16:13.

Christ also continued to speak through His apostles. In preparing them to meet the persecution and opposition which inevitably would come upon them as they carried the Gospel out through the world He said, "Settle it therefore in your hearts, not to meditate beforehand how to answer: for I will give you a mouth and wisdom, which all your adversaries shall not be able to withstand or to gainsay," Luke 21:14, 15. "We are ambassadors therefore on behalf of Christ," said Paul, "as though God were entreating by us: we beseech you on behalf of Christ, be ye reconciled to God," II Cor. 5:20. Thus the prophetic work of Christ continued as the Holy Spirit enlightened the Apostles and rendered them infallible in their capacity as teachers and as authors of the New Testament books, although that infallibility did not extend to their personal conduct nor to their personal ideas on other subjects. And while infallibility did not extend beyond the Apostles and some few of their immediate associates, ministers of the Gospel down through the ages are, in a secondary but nevertheless true sense, prophets prophesying in Christ's stead. They are His ambassadors. The Gospel ministry is therefore at once the most exalted and the most responsible office in the world. The prophetic work of Christ is also continued down through the ages as the Holy Spirit enlightens the minds of His people and leads them to understand spiritual truth which otherwise would be incomprehensible to them.

Furthermore, since Christ reveals the Father, and since the Father is infinite, His prophetic work will be endless. "These things have I spoken unto you in dark sayings: the hour cometh, when I shall no more speak unto you in dark sayings, but shall tell you plainly of the Father," John 16:25, said Jesus to His disciples shortly before He left them; and again, "I have yet many things to say unto you, but ye cannot bear them now," John 16:12. Indeed, as Dr. Strong very fittingly says: "In heaven Christ will be the visible God. We shall never see the Father separate from Christ. No man or angel has at any time seen God, 'whom no man hath seen, nor can see.' 'The only begotten Son. . . . He hath declared Him,' and He will forever declare Him (John 1:18; I Tim. 6:16)."[1]

2. CHRIST AS PRIEST

In answer to the question, "How doth Christ execute the office of a priest?" the Shorter Catechism says: "Christ executeth the office of a priest, in His once offering up of Himself a sacrifice to satisfy divine justice, and reconcile us to God, and in making continual intercession for us."

We have seen that a prophet is one who is qualified and authorized to speak for God to men. A priest, by way of contrast, is one who is qualified and authorized to treat in behalf of, or to represent men before the throne of God. Man in his fallen condition is a guilty sinner, in open and defiant rebellion against God. He therefore has neither the right nor even the desire to come into God's presence. A priest is one who, acting on man's behalf, undertakes to restore harmonious relations between God and man. In order to accomplish this he publicly acknowledges man's sin, offers gifts and sacrifices to God in order to expiate that sin and make God propitious, and then, having gained access to God, intercedes in man's behalf.

Since man in his fallen condition is blinded by sin, he does not realize the utter hopelessness of his condition. His ten-

---
1. *Systematic Theology*, p. 713.

dency is to put God out of his thoughts, to think that he is the master of his fate and the captain of his soul, and that he is able to turn from evil to good whenever he chooses. But his reasoning is based on utterly false premises. Hence if he is to be saved, it is necessary that God take the initiative and rescue him. And this, the Scriptures tell us, is precisely what God has done. Entirely at His own cost, and through pure grace alone, He has provided a system of redemption. "Christ died for the ungodly," says Paul, Rom. 5:6; and then he continues: "God commendeth His own love toward us, in that, while we were yet sinners, Christ died for us. Much more then, being now justified by His blood, shall we be saved from the wrath of God through Him. For if, while we were enemies, we were reconciled to God through the death of His Son, much more, being reconciled, shall we be saved by His life," Rom. 5:8-10.

The New Testament makes it plain that Christ is our Priest, our great High Priest. This function He performed in that He offered sacrifice and interceded effectively with God in our behalf. The supreme purpose of His coming, the writer of the Epistle to the Hebrews tells us, was "to put away sin by the sacrifice of Himself," 9:26. Specifically, He offered Himself through His suffering and death on the cross as a sacrifice to God to satisfy divine justice and reconcile us to God, and that in such a manner that He was at one and the same time the sacrifice and the priest who offered it. The Epistle to the Hebrews is in fact concerned almost exclusively with showing that He is our great High Priest and that it is through His sacrifice that our salvation has been made possible. "Having then a great High Priest, who hath passed through the heavens, Jesus the Son of God, let us hold fast our confession," Heb. 4:14. "For such a High Priest became us, holy, guiltless, undefiled, separated from sinners, and made higher than the heavens; who needeth not daily, like those high priests, to offer up sacrifices, first for his own sins, and then for the sins of the people: for this He did once for all, when He offered up Himself," Heb. 7:26, 27. "Thou art a priest for ever, after the order of Melchizedek," Heb. 5:6. The Old Testament priests, offering the blood of goats and bulls which had no saving power in itself, were required to offer their sacrifices repeatedly. "But Christ," we are told, "having come a high priest of the good things to come, through the greater and more perfect tabernacle, not made with hands, that is to say, not of this creation, nor yet through the blood of goats and calves, but through His own blood, entered in once for all into the holy place, having obtained eternal redemption. . . . For Christ entered not into a holy place made with hands, like in pattern to the true; but into heaven itself, now to appear before the face of God for us: nor yet that He should offer Himself often, as the high priest entereth into the holy place year by year with blood not his own; else must He often have suffered since the foundation of the world: but now once at the end of the ages hath He been manifested to put away sin by the sacrifice of Himself," Heb. 9:11, 12, 24-27. "Behold the man whose name is the Branch. . . . He shall be a priest upon His throne," said Zechariah (6:12, 13) as he predicted the advent of the Messiah and set Him forth as a royal priest. And Matthew tells us that "The Son of Man came not to be ministered unto, but to minister, and to give His life a ransom for many" (20:28). When viewed against the background of Jewish ritual and Old Testament sacrifice, it is perfectly clear that the death of Christ was designed to make possible the forgiveness of sin. The trail of blood that first appears outside the Garden of Eden leads unerringly to the cross on Calvary.

Furthermore, the priesthood of Christ did not cease with the completion of His work on earth, but continues for ever. His work of sacrifice was, of course, finished with His offering of Himself. But His work of intercession, which was begun on earth and which reached its climax in the high priestly prayer recorded in the seventeenth chapter of John, is continued in the presence of God as He fulfills this the second office of the priest. But He now prays not with strong crying and tears as in the days of His flesh (Heb. 5:7), but with the sovereignty and prevailing power of One who by His own work has achieved eternal redemption for His people. This intercession is repeatedly mentioned. In the Levitical system it was necessary that there be a succession of priests, "priests many in number, because that by death they are hindered from continuing: but He, because He abideth for ever, hath His priesthood unchangeable. Wherefore also He is able to save to the uttermost them that draw near unto God through Him, seeing He ever liveth to make intercession for them," Heb. 7:23-25. "If any man sin, we have an Advocate with the Father, Jesus Christ the righteous," said the Apostle John, I John 2:1. "It is Jesus Christ that died, yea rather, that was raised from the dead, who is at the right hand of God, who also maketh intercession for us," said Paul, Rom. 8:34. "He bare the sin of many, and made intercession for the transgressors," said Isaiah (53:12) in anticipation of the advent of the Messiah.

We have said that the Old Testament priests, like the Old Testament prophets, were but types and shadows of the Great One who was to come later. But while they were only types and shadows they had not, like the priests in the heathen religions, usurped their offices but were truly appointed by God. Their priesthood was effective in bringing salvation to men because it was a promise of, and pointed forward to, the one true Priest who on Calvary was to offer the only sacrifice that can take away the sins of men. And since the merely human priesthood was but a shadow of that which was to come, it was but temporary. Just as we put out our artificial lights when the sun rises, and as the blossom falls away when the fruit appears, so the entire ceremonial and sacrificial system of the Old Testament had fulfilled its function and ceased to be when Christ's work was completed. This being the nature of the Christian priesthood, it is clearly evident that all those today who, in the Roman Catholic or any other church, pretend to function as priests mediating between God and man are simply usurpers of divine authority.

3. CHRIST AS KING

The third office that Christ executes as our Redeemer is that of king. The Shorter Catechism, in answer to the question, "How doth Christ execute the office of a king?" says: "Christ executeth the office of a king, in subduing us to Himself, in ruling and defending us, and in restraining and conquering all His and our enemies."

The kingly office of Christ relates primarily to the risen and glorified Christ who, seated at the right hand of the Father and possessed of all authority in heaven and on earth, directs the advancing affairs of His kingdom and secures the salvation of His people. Exercising His authority through the agency of the Holy Spirit, through whom He is ever present with His people, He effectively applies to His people the redemption which He has worked out for them and effectively restrains the forces of evil which would thwart their redemption. As the Second Person of the Trinity Christ possessed divine power and glory from eternity, and so was King of the entire universe. But during the time of His career on earth He voluntarily subjected Himself to the limitations and privations of human nature, and His divine power and glory were veiled except for occasional miracles which bore testimony to the nature of His mission and work. But with the completion of His work of redemption He, as the God-Man, ascended to heaven in His glorified nature and now directs every step in the advancement of His kingdom.

That Christ is a king is taught clearly and repeatedly in Scripture. In the first place His name, "Christ," means "anointed." In Old Testament times the anointing of the king signified his appointment to the kingly office. To Samuel God said, "Fill thy horn with oil, and go: I will send thee to Jesse, the Bethlehemite; for I have provided me a king among his sons. . . . Then Samuel took the horn of oil, and anointed him in the midst of his brethren: and the Spirit of Jehovah came mightily upon David from that day forward," I Sam. 16:1,13. After announcing to Mary that she should have a Son whose name was to be called Jesus, the angel Gabriel added: "He shall be great, and shall be called the Son of the Most High: and the Lord God shall give unto Him the throne of His father David: and He shall reign over the house of Jacob for ever and ever; and of His kingdom there shall be no end," Luke 1:32,33. At the very beginning of His public ministry Nathanael, impressed with His supernatural insight, acknowledged His true kingship: "Rabbi, thou art the Son of God, thou art King of Israel," John 1:49. Christ Himself claimed to be a king, and announced the establishment of His kingdom, which is variously called the kingdom of heaven, the kingdom of God, the kingdom of Christ. Mark tells us that early in His ministry, "Jesus came into Galilee, preaching the Gospel of God, saying, The time is fulfilled, and the kingdom of God is at hand: repent ye, and believe the Gospel," 1:14,15. In the Sermon on the Mount He made it plain that not mere lip service but only true allegiance from the

The Offices of Christ 183

heart would secure admittance into His kingdom: "Not every one that saith unto me, Lord, Lord, shall enter into the kingdom of heaven; but he that doeth the will of my Father who is in heaven," Matt. 7:21. In the eschatological discourse of Matt. 25:31-46 Christ pictured Himself as seated upon the throne of universal judgment, before whom is to be gathered all the nations, whose voice pronounces sentence and assigns to the good and the evil their eternal rewards and punishments. In conformity with the accepted custom of the Roman Empire that the newly designated king, coming to the capital city for the first time in his official capacity, should be mounted on a proud spirited horse and publicly welcomed by a multitude of his people who shouted his praise and strewed flowers in his path, Jesus so entered Jerusalem on Palm Sunday, except that instead of the proud spirited horse he used the lowly ass, symbol of service and humility,—thus literally fulfilling the words of the prophet Zechariah: "Rejoice greatly, O daughter of Zion; shout, O daughter of Jerusalem: behold, thy King cometh unto thee; He is just, and having salvation; lowly, and riding upon an ass, even upon a colt the foal of an ass," Zech. 9:9; Matt. 21:5. On this same occasion He was welcomed by the crowd with the words, "Blessed is the King that cometh in the name of the Lord," Luke 19:38,—which welcome He accepted as entirely appropriate. During His trial before Pilate His enemies made the charge: "We found this man . . . saying that He Himself is Christ a king," Luke 23:2. In reply to Pilate's question Jesus said: "My kingdom is not of this world: if my kingdom were of this world, then would my servants fight, that I should not be delivered to the Jews: but now is my kingdom not from hence," John 18:36; and when asked directly, "Are thou a king then?" He answered affirmatively: "Thou sayest that I am a king. To this end have I been born, and to this end am I come into the world, that I should bear witness unto the truth," John 18:37.

Paul's testimony to the kingship of Christ is, of course, clear and abundant. In the Epistle to the Ephesians he declares that "God raised Him from the dead, and made Him to sit at His right hand in the heavenly places, far above all rule, and authority, and power, and dominion, and every name that is named, not only in this world, but also in that which is to come: and He put all things in subjection under His feet, and gave Him to be head over all things to the Church," 1:20-23. To sit at the right hand of the Father is to occupy the position of honor and power. In these words Paul tells us that Christ, in His theanthropic nature, now presides at the tribunal of heaven, that all creatures, celestial and terrestrial, admire His majesty, obey His will, and are subject to His power. In the Epistle to the Philippians he declares that "God highly exalted Him, and gave unto Him the name which is above every name; that in the name of Jesus every knee should bow, of things in heaven and things on earth and things under the earth, and that every tongue should confess that Jesus Christ is Lord, to the glory of God the Father," 2:9-11. In First Corinthians he says that "He must reign, till He hath put all His enemies under His feet," 15:25. And in First Timothy he declares that Christ is "the blessed and only Potentate, the King of kings, and Lord of lords," 6:15.

In Heb. 2:8,9 we read: "For in that He subjected all things unto Him, He left nothing that is not subject to Him. But now we see not yet all things subjected to Him. But we behold . . . Jesus . . . crowned with glory and honor." And in Heb. 1:8 the 45th Psalm is quoted as having its fulfillment in Christ: "Thy throne, O God, is for ever and ever;

The Offices of Christ 185

and the sceptre of uprightness is the sceptre of thy kingdom."

The book of Revelation is one sustained hymn of praise to Christ as King, setting forth the glory of His person and the triumph of His kingdom. He is declared to be "the Ruler of the kings of the earth," 1:5. He has "made us to be a kingdom, to be priests unto His God and Father; to Him be the glory and the dominion for ever and ever," 1:5. In chapter 5 He is pictured as sitting on the throne and receiving homage and worship from all the hosts of heaven and earth. All opposition is to be utterly crushed: "and out of His mouth proceedeth a sharp sword, that with it He should smite the nations: and He shall rule them with a rod of iron. . . . And He hath on His garment and on His thigh a name written, KING OF KINGS, AND LORD OF LORDS," 19:15, 16,—not that He will use violence or military force, but rather that His conquest of the nations is to be accomplished by the preaching of the Gospel, as is indicated by the fact that the sword proceeds "out of His mouth;" and, continuing with the same figure of speech, while it will be an immeasurable pleasure and privilege for His people to be ruled by Him, His rule will be as complete and effective as if enforced with a rod of iron.

The Old Testament too sets forth His kingship. The predicted Messiah is set forth as the King of the Golden Age in which the wolf and the lamb lay down together, Is. 11:1-10. In the Messianic vision recorded in Daniel 7:13,14 we read: "There came with the clouds of heaven one like unto a Son of Man, and He came even to the Ancient of Days, and they brought Him near before Him. And there was given Him dominion, and glory, and a kingdom, that all the peoples, nations, and languages should serve Him: His dominion is an everlasting dominion, which shall not pass away, and His kingdom that which shall not be destroyed." The Messianic psalms strongly emphasize the kingly nature of the coming One, some making special mention of His conquest of the wicked: "I have set my King upon my holy hill in Zion," 2:6; "Thy throne, O God, is for ever and ever" (quoted in Heb. 1:8 as having its fulfillment in Christ); "Ask of me, and I will give thee the nations for thine inheritance, and the uttermost parts of the earth for thy possession. Thou shalt break them with a rod of iron; Thou shalt dash them in pieces like a potter's vessel," Ps. 2:8,9; "Jehovah saith unto my Lord, Sit thou at my right hand, until I make thine enemies thy footstool," Ps. 110:1 (quoted five times in the New Testament as having its fulfillment in Christ).

The inward spiritual nature of His kingdom as well as its present existence was set forth by Christ Himself when, being asked by the Pharisees concerning the time of its appearance, He said, "The kingdom of God cometh not with observation" —that is, not with outward and spectacular signs or events— "neither shall they say, Lo, here! or There! for lo, the kingdom of God is within you," Luke 17:21,22. The kingdoms of this world are established with mighty armies, great conquests, violence and cruelty. But how different was the advent of Jesus, without earthly eminence, without arms, without wealth. Individuals are brought into His kingdom one by one as the Holy Spirit regenerates their hearts and implants a new principle of spiritual life. The Christian, although in the world, is no longer of it. Actuated by new motives and new desires and acknowledging Christ as His only Lord and Master, he looks forward to a new heavens and a new earth wherein dwelleth righteousness. Paul fittingly says that "our citizenship is in heaven," Phil 3:20.

The writer of the Epistle to the Hebrews, after having called the roll of the outstanding faithful, says that these "confessed that they were strangers and pilgrims on the

The Offices of Christ

earth," 11:13, and later adds that "we have not here an abiding city, but we seek after the city which is to come," 13:14, —"the city which hath the foundations, whose builder and maker is God," 11:10. The visible representation of the kingdom on earth is, of course, the Church, in so far as the Church is composed of true believers.

In order to make clear the nature of Christ's kingdom in its broadest outlines it probably can be best presented under three heads: *The Kingdom of Power; The Kingdom of Grace;* and, *The Kingdom of Glory.*

(1). *Christ's Kingdom of Power* relates to the universe at large as, by virtue of His Divine nature and His work of creatorship, He upholds (that is, preserves in existence) all things visible and invisible, governs (throughout the realm of nature as well as in the affairs of men), and passes final judgment on the entire race of men. That He was the active agent, although not the exclusive agent, in the creation of all things is repeatedly taught in Scripture: "All things were made through Him; and without Him was not anything made that hath been made . . . the world was made through Him," John 1:3,10; "Through whom also He made the worlds," Heb. 1:2; "All things have been created through Him, and unto Him; and He is before all things, and in Him all things consist," Col. 1:16,17. He rules or governs all things, for the glory of God and the effective execution of the divine plan: "All authority hath been given unto me in heaven and on earth," Matt. 28:18; "Wherefore also God highly exalted Him, and gave unto Him the name which is above every name; that in the name of Jesus every knee should bow, of things in heaven and things on earth and things under the earth, and that every tongue should confess that Jesus Christ is Lord, to the glory of God the Father," Phil 2:9-11; "The exceeding greatness of His power . . . which He (that is,

God the Father) wrought in Christ, when He raised Him from the dead, and made Him to sit at His right hand in the heavenly places, far above all rule, and authority, and power, and dominion, and every name that is named, not only in this world, but also in that which is to come: and He put all things in subjection under His feet, and gave Him to be the head over all things in the Church," Eph. 1:19-22; "For in that He subjected all things unto Him, He left nothing that is not subject to Him. But now we see not yet all things subject to Him. But we behold . . . Jesus . . . crowned with glory and honor," Heb. 2:8,9. And that He is to be the final Judge of all men is set forth with equal clearness: "But when the Son of Man shall come in His glory, and all the angels with Him, then shall He sit on the throne of His glory: and before Him shall be gathered all the nations. . . . Then shall the King say unto them on His right hand, Come, ye blessed of my Father, inherit the kingdom prepared for you from the foundation of the world. . . . Then shall He say also unto them on the left hand, Depart from me, ye cursed, into the eternal fire which is prepared for the Devil and his angels," Matt. 25:31-41. His conquest of the nations, which is to be accomplished through the preaching of the Gospel, and His effective government of them in righteousness is foretold in figurative language in the book of Revelation: ". . . Upon His head are many diadems. . . . And the armies which are in heaven followed Him upon white horses, clothed in fine linen, pure and white. And out of His mouth proceedeth a sharp sword, that with it He should smite the nations: and He shall rule them with a rod of iron. . . And He hath on His garment and on His thigh a name written, KING OF KINGS, AND LORD OF LORDS," 19:15, 16. Thus His kingdom of power embraces the material world, the course of history, and all angels and men.

The Offices of Christ

(2). *The Kingdom of Grace.* Christ's Kingdom of Grace is that spiritual kingdom in which He rules in the hearts and lives of believers. It is a kingdom which is here and now: "The kingdom of God is within you," Luke 17:20. It was originally founded by Him, being made possible by His atoning work on the cross. It receives its laws from Him. In all ages He administers its affairs and defends it against all enemies. Its membership on earth is identical with that of the true Church, which is composed of all those who from the heart believe in Christ as Saviour and Lord. It is a kingdom which is in the world but not of it: "They are not of the world, even as I am not of the world," John 17:16, "If ye were of the world, the world would love its own: but because ye are not of the world, but I chose you out of the world, therefore the world hateth you," John 15:19; "My kingdom is not of this world: if my kingdom were of this world, then would my servants fight, that I should not be delivered to the Jews: but now is my kingdom not from hence," John 18:36. Its distinguishing characteristics are not earthly or carnal: "For the kingdom of God is not eating and drinking, but righteousness and peace and joy in the Holy Spirit," Rom. 14:17. It is made effective, not by any external display of power or magnificence, but by a divine work of the Holy Spirit as He regenerates the hearts and gives spiritual insight to the minds of men: "The kingdom of God cometh not with observation," Luke 17:20; "Except one be born anew, he cannot see the kingdom of God," John 3:3; "Not by works done in righteousness, which we did ourselves, but according to His mercy He saved us, through the washing of regeneration and renewing of the Holy Spirit," Titus 3:5. But while the coming of the kingdom is not heralded by external signs, its effect within the individual is immediately felt in that he becomes conscious of a new relationship to God and of new governing principles which make for holiness, sobriety and uprightness; and in due time the eflects thus wrought in individuals are reflected in the improved social, economic and political conditions of the whole communty or nation.

Christ's kingdom of grace embraces all types of men, recognizing no distinctions of nationality, color, class, rank, person or sex. "There can be neither Jew nor Greek, there can be neither bond nor free, there can be no male and female; for ye are all one man in Christ Jesus," says Paul, Gal. 3:28. That it was not intended for the Jews alone but for all nations and races was set forth clearly in the Old Testament Messianic passages and was repeatedly emphasized in the New Testament: "Ask of me, and I will give thee the nations for thine inheritance, And the uttermost parts of the earth for thy possession," Ps. 2:8; "I will also give thee for a light to the Gentiles, that thou mayest be my salvation unto the end of the earth," Is. 49:6; "From the rising of the sun even unto the going down of the same my name shall be great among the Gentiles," Mal. 1:11; "I will give thee for a covenant of the people, for a light of the Gentiles," Is. 42:6; "And it shall come to pass afterward that I will pour out my Spirit upon all flesh," Joel 2:28. When the infant Jesus was presented in the temple the aged but spiritually minded Simeon recognized Him as "A light for revelation to the Gentiles, And the glory of thy people Israel," Luke 2:32. "Of a truth I perceive that God is no respecter of persons: but in every nation he that feareth Him, and worketh righteousness, is acceptable to Him," said Peter when he realized the full meaning of the vision he had seen while on the housetop, Acts 10:34, 35. "Is God the God of Jews only? is He not the God of Gentiles also? Yea, of Gentiles also," said Paul, Rom. 3:29. And the last command of

Christ to His disciples was, "Go ye therefore, and make disciples of all the nations," Matt. 28:19.

We wish particularly to stress the fact that Christ is in the truest sense of the word our King today, that, having established His Church as the fellowship of believers, He now is seated on the throne of the universe from whence He directs the affairs of His advancing kingdom, that He animates His people with new spiritual life and defends them against all the forces of evil, and that He is thus to continue until all His enemies have been placed under His feet. It is our duty never to despair of the Church, nor of the world, which eventually is to be conquered by the Church. Since the Kingdom of Grace is not terrestial or carnal, but spiritual, we must not be surprised if during our course through a world in which there still remains so much that is evil we often suffer persecutions, sickness, poverty, cold, hunger, and other disagreeable circumstances. For all of these things have their appointed place in God's providential control of the world, and as they come upon believers they are designed not as punishments but as disciplines or chastisements for their improvement. We have the assurance of our King that He will never forsake us—"Lo, I am with you always, even unto the end of the world"—and that He will supply, not our every desire, but our "every need . . . according to His riches in glory," Phil. 4:19. Being truly united with Christ and depending on the power of His Spirit, we shall not doubt but that we shall be finally victorious over the Devil and every kind of evil that he can bring against us. We look upon science, education, invention, art, music, commerce, statesmanship, sociology, etc., each in its own field so far as it is based on truth, as a revelation of the wisdom and glory of Christ, who is the Light of the world and the Ruler of the nations. Each of these represents an accomplishment in man's conquest of the forces of nature, which was the task assigned to him when immediately after his creation he was commanded to "subdue" the earth; and each of these is a prophecy of the complete establishment of Christ's kingdom. Let us ever remember that Christ is our King here and now, that He is ruling and overruling through the whole course of human history, making the wrath of men to praise Him and able even to bring good out of that which men intend for evil.

And since Christ is thus our King it is our duty in every sphere of life's activity to render to Him that homage and obedience which is His due. In the following paragraph Dr. Craig sets forth this obligation very clearly. "It is important," says he, "that we note the all-inclusiveness of Christ's rule. Not only does He demand obedience from all men; He demands obedience from them in all things. . . . There is no sphere of life conceivable where Jesus does not maintain His demand that He be honored and obeyed. As King, therefore, Christ ought to be supreme in our private lives. Within this sphere we ought to strive to bring every thought and activity into captivity to Him. As King, Christ's will ought, also, to be supreme in our social and business lives. Within these spheres we should be guided by the golden rule; we should place the emphasis upon our duties rather than upon our rights. Still further, as King, Christ's will ought to be supreme in our political lives. To deny this is tantamount to saying that politics ought to be Christless. This is not to say that the Church, as an institution, ought to mix in politics, but it is to say that, if we are Christians, our Christianity will manifest itself in the sphere of politics as well as in the other spheres of life. Let us not imagine, then, that Christ's kingship has to do with only a part of life; it has to do with the whole life. Wherever we may be, whatever we may do, in the world of action or of thought, we are under

The Offices of Christ

the dominion of, and as such responsible to, Jesus Christ."[2]

Furthermore, whether in human or divine affairs, the relationship between king and subjects is a reciprocal relation. Not only do the subjects have obligations toward their king, but the king also has obligations toward his subjects. In this connection Dr. Craig has said: "For our comfort and encouragement let us remind ourselves that—assuming that we are endeavoring to yield Him that obedience that is His due—Christ has placed Himself under obligations to us. As subjects of the King we do, indeed, owe Him homage and obedience. At the same time, however, He, as our King, grants us support and protection. What holds good of our relations to the State holds good, in a true sense, of our relations to King Jesus. As long as we obey the laws of the State, the State will protect and defend us. If others seek to take away our life, our liberty or our possessions we are not dependent upon our own resources: all the resources of the State are pledged for the support and defense of even the weakest and most insignificant of its citizens. And so as long as we serve Jesus as King, all His power and strength is pledged to our support and defense. No matter how weak and helpless we may be in ourselves; no matter how strong and reliant they may be who are against us, we need not fear, for greater is He that is for us than they that be against us. No doubt, if left to ourselves, we would soon be overcome of evil; but as it is King Jesus watches over us and defends us, and thus we are enabled to prevail not because of our own strength but because of the strength of Him in whom we have put our trust. Let us then be of good cheer. Though all the hosts of earth and hell should conspire together to accomplish the undoing of the weakest of Christ's true subjects they would not succeed. Unto Him that watches over

---

2. *Jesus As He Was and Is*, p. 84.

us and defends us has been committed all power and authority in heaven and on earth."[3]

Today Christ's kingship is, of course, widely ignored. In this connection we find another valuable comment in the writings of Dr. Craig. Says he: "Everywhere there are those who say by their actions if not by their words that they do not recognize His right to rule over them. It is necessary, therefore, to distinguish between His *de facto* and His *de iure* rule, i.e., between the obedience that is actually yielded Him and the obedience that is His by law and right. According to law and right Jesus is entitled to universal obedience. As a matter of fact only a relatively few render Him the homage and obedience that is His due. We may be sure, however, that things will not always remain as they are in this respect. Jesus being what He is we may be confident that He will make good His claims and that the time is coming when all men, willingly or unwillingly, will acknowledge His lordship. Let no one suppose that Jesus' right to rule rests on the consent of men, that He exercises rightful authority only over those who acknowledge His lordship. It is not for you or for me, it is not for any man to say, whether he will live in Christ's kingdom. This is true, in some degree at least, of the kingdoms of this world. If we do not like the way in which authority is exercised in that one in which we happen to be, we may move to one more to our liking. Nothing like this is possible, however, in connection with the kingdom of Christ. His kingdom is not confined to any special territory. Go where we may, we are still within His jurisdiction and answerable to His authority. We might as well suppose that we can go where the law of gravitation does not operate as suppose we can go where Christ does not hold sway. Hence just as it is the part of wisdom to adjust our-

---
3. *Craig*, p. 85.

The Offices of Christ

selves to the law of gravitation so that it will operate for our advantage and not to our disadvantage, it is the part of wisdom to adjust ourselves to the Lord Jesus in such a way that His rule will bring us weal not woe, gain not loss, life not death."[4]

That Christ does exist as King is recognized by Roman Catholics as well as by Protestants—a fact which could hardly be denied since it is set forth so clearly in Scripture—although they differ quite radically in regard to the manner in which He exercises His authority. Roman Catholics hold that He has appointed the Pope as His vice-regent on earth, and that His kingly authority is thus exercised through the instrumentality of a human being. We hold, however, with the whole Protestant world that not only is there no Scripture authority to support such a claim but that such a claim is contrary to the plain teaching of Scripture, and that the authority by which the Pope presumes to speak and act in the name of Christ is simply usurped authority. We hold that every believer is directly responsible to King Jesus Himself, and that it is our God-given right to go directly to Him in prayer without the intervention of any earthly pope or hierarchy. Our conviction in this regard is only strengthened when we examine more closely into the private lives and conduct of many of the popes and priests who have presumed to exercise this authority. A church which has incorporated so much error into its teaching and which has engaged in such shameless oppressions and persecutions as has the Roman Catholic Church is plainly not the authorized agency of Christ on earth.

In this treatment we have given undue space to the Kingdom of Grace, since that is the phase of Christ's kingdom in which we now are, and since it is also the phase concerning

---
4. *Craig*, p. 82.

196   *The Person of Christ*

which we have the most information. There is, however, a third phase, and we must now turn our attention to that.

(3). *The Kingdom of Glory.* Christ's Kingdom of Glory is that state in which He rules over the redeemed in heaven and over the holy angels. It began with His ascension, and it reaches its consummation and completion at the end of the world and the final judgment. Entrance into the Kingdom of Glory is through the Kingdom of Grace; and it grows and develops as the members of the Church Militant, one by one, are translated into the Church Triumphant. In anticipation of his estate in this kingdom Paul wrote to the Philippians, "For me to live is Christ, and to die is gain," 1:21; and in the same connection he declared that he had "the desire to depart and to be with Christ," which, said he, "is very far better," Phil. 1:23. John pronounces blessed those who are privileged to share in the glories of this kingdom: "Blessed are the dead who die in the Lord," Rev. 14:13. In the highly figurative passage of Rev. 20:4-6 John gives us an insight into the joys experienced by those who are privileged to share in this kingdom as, released from all earthly cares and limitations, they "lived, and reigned with Christ a thousand years,"—which period of time, we believe, is to be understood not as an exact one thousand years but a comparatively long period, specifically, as relates to each individual, the period between his death here and the consummation of the kingdom at the end of the world. For some of the redeemed, perhaps for most of them, this period will continue much longer than a literal one thousand years. All of those who have suffered and died for Christ, that is, all of those who in one way or another have given their lives in Christian service, are described as having been "beheaded for the testimony of Jesus and for the word of God," Rev. 21:4. If this be taken literally to include only those martyrs who actually have been beheaded, to the exclusion of all those who have been burned at the stake or who have suffered torture or privation in other ways, the number partaking of the joys of this reign would be relatively insignificant. As a matter of fact many of those who have been put to death by being beheaded have suffered much less than those who have died by other means, or who after a life of Christian service have died natural deaths. Consequently we understand this to mean that all those who have suffered for Christ have a part in His mediatorial reign. Furthermore, as these persons are awaiting the resurrection they are in a disembodied state and are described not as men and women but as "souls," and their estate there is figuratively described as "the first resurrection." It is an inestimable privilege to share in this intermediate reign, and those who are thus privileged are described as "blessed and holy." "Over these," John tells us, "the second death"—by which he evidently means the state of torture into which the wicked are to be cast—"hath no power; but they shall be priests of God and of Christ; and shall reign with Him a thousand years," Rev. 20:6. Furthermore, when seen in this light death should hold no horrors for the Christian, but should be looked upon primarily as a transition from this world to Christ's Kingdom of Glory, or as the gateway through which he enters a far better and more glorious life than can ever be attained here.

The mediatorial reign of Christ closes with His second coming and the final judgment. The work of redemption then will have been completed, divine grace will have been fully manifested, and the fate of all men, good or bad, fixed forever. Then Christ, having gained the complete victory and having reigned till He has put all His enemies under His feet, shall deliver up the kingdom to God the Father, ". . . that God may be all in all," I Cor. 15:23-28. This does not mean that from that time on Christ will cease to have any part in the kingdom, but that, the work of redemption having been completed and the elect gathered in, it will cease to be pre-eminently His kingdom, that He will return to the original relationship which He had with the Father and the Holy Spirit, and that the triune God will reign eternally over the perfected kingdom.

In conclusion, then, Christ is at one and the same time our Prophet, our Priest, and our King. This is the terminology under which His work is set forth in Scripture. It is to John Calvin that we are indebted for developing more clearly than anyone else had done this threefold nature of the work of redemption. But while we use this terminology we are not to assume that these are separate offices as are those of President, Chief Justice and Senator in the affairs of State, or that these functions are performed successively and in isolation. Rather they are concurrent and mutually imply one another as do lungs, heart and brain in the human body — functionally distinct, yet interdependent and together constituting the one life. With varying degrees of emphasis Christ is always a royal Priest, a priestly King, a priestly Prophet, and a prophetical Priest. His work as Prophet, through which He reveals God to us, is rightly understood only when we know Him as the One who through His priestly work has redeemed us and who is our heavenly King. His work as Priest—His offering up Himself as a sacrifice to satisfy divine justice and reconcile us to God—is made known to us through His work as prophet as He reveals to us the true meaning of His suffering and death. And His work as King can be rightly understood only when through His work as Prophet He reveals Himself as the One who has purchased us with His own blood, whose possession therefore we are.

The Offices of Christ

In the typical economy of Israel's long history there were three distinct offices, that of the prophet, of the priest, and of the king. In the historical order the prophetic order was established first. Abraham was a prophet (Gen. 20:6); Jacob performed this function (Gen. 49:1); and Moses was officially called to be a prophet before he led the Children of Israel out of Egypt. The priests were appointed soon after Israel became a nation. The kings, however, did not begin to reign until some four hundred years later, Israel in the meantime existing as a theocracy in which God as their King governed through the prophets. As the Old Testament prophets were types of the great Prophet, and the Old Testament priests were types of the great Priest, so were the Old Testament kings types of the great King. The three functions which ran in separate though parallel lines during Old Testament times were thus merged and brought to perfection in Christ. But even in Him the emphasis on the three offices still fell in the historical order, so that during His public ministry He acted primarily as Prophet; in His suffering and death on the cross and in His intercession for us before the throne of God He acted primarily as Priest; and in His Kingdom of Grace and His Kingdom of Glory He has revealed Himself primarily as King

Furthermore, as a result of Christ's work of redemption, all believers, under the New Covenant, are made prophets, priests and kings. We are constituted prophets in that we are commanded to proclaim the Gospel and to show forth the excellencies of Him who called us out of darkness into His marvelous light (Matt. 28:18). Peter sets forth the priesthood when he says, "Ye are an elect race, a royal priesthood, a holy nation, a people for God's own possession," I Peter 2:9; and likewise John when he says, "He made us to be a kingdom, to be priests unto His God and Father," Rev. 1:6.

And the kingly estate of the Lord's people is set forth when Peter declares that believers are a "royal" priesthood, and when John declares that those in the intermediate state "shall reign with Him a thousand years," Rev. 20:6, and that those in heaven "shall reign for ever and ever," Rev. 22:5. Thus the three offices which for centuries ran parallel in Israel and then were united in the Lord Jesus Christ reappear in all those who believe in Him. Each believer ideally and potentially has all three offices. Some are pre-eminently prophets in that they proclaim the Gospel. Others are preeminently priests, not that they offer any more sacrifices for sin, for Christ alone offered that sacrifice, but in that they minister under their great High Priest and offer up for themselves and others spiritual sacrifices, which sacrifices include (1) themselves as living sacrifices in service to God, (2) their possessions, (3) prayer, (4) praise, and (5) thanksgiving. And while the kingly office is largely reserved for the future, some even in this life through the instrumentality of their office in Church or State exercise authority over their fellow men.

XXII.

ERRONEOUS VIEWS CONCERNING THE PERSON OF CHRIST

IN ORDER that we may keep more clearly in mind the true doctrine concerning the person of Christ it may be helpful to make a brief survey of the erroneous views that have emerged during the course of Church history. As we have stated at the very beginning of this study, the first question that must be settled by anyone professing to be a Christian is, "What think ye of the Christ?" (Matt. 22:42); and as that question is answered the truth or falsity of that person's Christianity becomes evident. As a matter of historical record the full statement concerning the person of Christ was arrived at only after protracted and violent controversies, during the course of which every possible interpretation of the biblical data was examined, its elements of truth sifted out and preserved while the elements of error which deformed it were exposed and discarded.

1. EBIONISM

The earliest heretical view concerning the person of Christ was that known as "Ebionism." In the interests of a supposedly pure monotheism the Ebionites denied the Deity of Christ and held that He was merely a man on whom the Spirit of God rested in its fulness. God and man were regarded as always external to each other. It denied the possibility of a union of the divine and the human nature and so ruled out the doctrine of the Incarnation. Some Ebionites acknowledged His supernatural birth, while others rejected it and held that His baptism marked the time at which He was especially endowed with the Holy Spirit. All agreed that after His death He was exalted to kingship. But this means that they acknowledged Him only as a great prophet or teacher during His earthly career and so definitely a part of the creaturely existence,—all of which in turn means that the worship paid Him by the Church was simply idolatry. They held that the old Jewish law was still obligatory upon the Lord's people. Hence their system appears to have been simply Judaism within the pale of the Christian Church.

2. DOCETISM

Chronologically, the next important error to develop concerning the person of Christ was Docetism. This term was derived from the Greek word *dokeo,* meaning to "seem," or to "appear." While the Ebionites believed that Christ had only a human nature, the Doceti held precisely the opposite error, asserting that He had only a divine nature and that His appearance in this world was only an illusion, or, more correctly, a theophany. According to this view He did not have a real human body and therefore could not have had a real human life. This meant further that He suffered no real pain and died no real death.

This peculiar belief was based on the philosophical assumption that matter is inherently evil. Since Christ was acknowledged to be altogether pure they could not admit that He was in any way connected with a physical body. Docetism was therefore simply pagan philosophy within the Church. It appeared, quite early, about the year A. D. 70, and continued for approximately a century. The Patripassion and Sabellian heresies which appeared later may well be considered sects of the Docetic heresy since they too denied any real humanity in Christ.

Erroneous Views Concerning the Person of Christ 203

The Scripture refutation of Docetism is found in John's declaration that "The Word became flesh, and dwelt among us (and we beheld His glory, glory as of the only begotten from the Father), full of grace and truth," 1:14; and also in the unequivocal statement of Heb. 2:14: "Since then the children are sharers in flesh and blood, He also Himself in like manner partook of the same." Incidentally we may add that the early appearance of Docetism with its strong emphasis on the Deity of Christ is eloquent testimony showing that the impression made upon those who saw and heard Him in the flesh was that He was a supernatural Being.

3. ARIANISM

A third error that arose in the early Church, more serious than either of the preceding ones, was Arianism. This view denied the true Deity of Christ and held rather that He occupied a position somewhere between that of God and man, that He was the first created being and the creator of all other creatures. He was thus regarded not as possessing absolute Deity, but only as the highest of created beings. Because of the claims which He made, the authority which He assumed, the miracles He worked, and the glory He displayed particularly in His resurrection, the great majority of the early Christians recognized Him as truly God. The Arians, however, misinterpreted certain Scripture statements relating to His state of humiliation and assumed that temporary subordination to the Father meant original and permanent inequality. Origen, the most outstanding of the early church fathers, in connection with his doctrine of the eternal generation of the Son, had taught inherent subordination. Arius carried this idea much farther and declared that the generation of the Sea had taken place in time, thus definitely making Him a creature.

In another connection the present writer has said concerning the Arian controversy: "This controversy was brought to a head in the early part of the fourth century by the teaching of Arius, a presbyter in the Church at Alexandria, Egypt. Because of the widespread difference of opinion concerning the person of Christ an Eucumenical Council was called by the first Christian Emperor, Constantine, for the purpose of formulating a general doctrine which should be accepted by the whole Church. The council met in the year 325, at Nicæa, in Asia Minor, and was attended by bishops and presbyters from practically all parts of the empire. The real controversy centered around the question as to whether Christ was to be considered as truly God, or as only the first and greatest creature. The Arians maintained that Christ was not eternal, that He was created by the Father out of nothing and was therefore the first and highest of all creatures, that He in turn created the world, and that because of the power delegated to Him He is to be looked upon as God and is to be worshipped. He was, therefore, to be called God only by courtesy, in much the same way that we give a Lieutenant Governor the title of Governor. His preeminence was due to the fact that He alone was created immediately by God and that supernatural power was given to Him, while all other creatures were created by Him. Most of the Arians also held that the Holy Spirit was the first and greatest of the creatures called into existence by His power. All of this meant, of course, a God who had a beginning, and who might therefore have an end; for a creature, no matter how highly exalted, must ever remain finite. Hence the Arians, in demanding worship of Christ, were in fact asserting the central principle of heathenism and idolatry, the worship of a creature.

"The Arians asserted that Christ was not of the same substance (*homo-ousia*) with the Father, but of similar substance (*homoi-ousia*). We may be tempted today to wonder how the whole Christian world could have been convulsed over the rejection of a single letter of the alphabet; but in reality the absence or the presence of the *iota* signified the difference between a Saviour who is truly God and one who is only a creature,—between a Christianity which is able to save the souls of men and one which can not. In the Council of Nicæa the Church faced what we believe to have been the greatest crisis in the entire history of doctrine. It was, however, in effect, although in a slightly different form, the same question that it faces in the twentieth century dispute between the Evangelical Faith and Modernism .

"The noble champion of the orthodox cause was Athanasius, who later became Bishop of Alexandria. Under His influence the Council declared for the full and eternal Deity of Christ, who was declared to be 'God of God, Light of Light, Very God of Very God, being of one substance with the Father.' Opposition continued strong for some time after the Council had made this pronouncement, but under the zealous and skillful leadership of Athanasius the doctrine gradually won official acceptance by the entire Church. It was seen that a created Christ was not the Christ of the New Testament, nor could He be the Christ who, by His death and resurrection, became the Author of eternal salvation."[1]

4. APOLLINARIANISM

The next error that the Church had to face concerning the person of Christ was that of Apollinarianism. This system denied the completeness of His human nature. It acknowledged His true Deity, and also that He possessed a real body

---
1. Article on The Trinity, *The Evangelical Quarterly*, London, Jan. 1939.

and a soul which would continue after death; but it denied that He had a truly human mind, i.e., a reasoning mind that reached conclusions through mental processes as do ours. It asserted in effect that He was simply God masquerading in human flesh, and that ignorance, weakness, obedience, worship, suffering, etc., were to be predicated of the Logos, that is, of the Deity or Divine nature as such. If, by way of comparison, we can imagine a man's mind implanted in the body of a lion and the lion thereafter governed not by lion or animal psychology but by a human mind we shall have something analogous to what the Apollinarian system set forth concerning the incarnation of Christ. Apollinarius was a tricotomist, and his system was based on the assumption that there were three elements in man's nature: a material body, an immortal soul, and a reasoning mind. We believe, however, that man is composed of only two elements, body and soul, and that the mind with which man reasons in this life is the same as the soul or spirit which lives on after death. Hence it is evident that, reduced to dicotomist terms, Apollinarianism granted Christ a human body but not a complete human soul. But if Christ was to have a real incarnation it was necessary that He add to His divine nature not merely a human body but also a human mind or soul; for humanity consists not merely in the possession of a body but of a body and soul. Apollinarianism was plainly an inconsistent explanation of the person of Christ, and it was condemned by the Council at Constantinople in the year 381.

5. NESTORIANISM

Another error that had a widespread influence in the early Church, ranking next to Arianism in importance and even resulting in a considerable portion of the Church splitting off from the main body, was that of Nestorianism. The error of Nestorius was that he carried the dual nature of Christ too far. This gave Christ a double personality, two natures and two persons instead of two natures and one person. Christ was thus regarded as a man in very close union with God, and Nestorius' favorite analogy to explain the person of Christ was that of the union of the believer with Christ. This, however, gave us not an incarnate God, but only a deified man,—one who came from below, not from above. Far from giving us a real incarnation, this system gave us only an alliance between God and a man. Somewhat after the fashion of the Siamese twins, Chang and Eng, God and man were joined together.

We have insisted repeatedly, of course, that Christ is an unique person, that in Him true Deity and true humanity are joined to form one person, and that He is as truly God as is God the Father and as truly man as we are. But we have also pointed out that there is nothing in Scripture to indicate that He was conscious of a double personality. It was not a man but manhood, that is, impersonal generic human nature, that He took into union with Himself. Since He had two natures He also had two wills, the human, however, being always in perfect harmony with and subordinate to the divine. This latter aspect of His personality was best illustrated in His prayer, "Not my will but thine be done." We are thus able to distinguish, but not to divide, the two natures in Christ. The chief error of the Nestorian system was that in separating the divine and the human natures in Christ it deprived His human sufferings of the value and efficacy that they must have if they are to be sufficient for the redemption of mankind. As we have pointed out earlier, only when His divine and human nature are organically and indissolubly united in one person can the acts of either nature have the value of both. Hence we are always to insist upon His true Deity, His true humanity, and the unity of His person.

6. EUTYCHIANISM

Perhaps the most peculiar of all of the Christological heresies was that of Eutychianism. This teaching denied the distinction between the divine and the human nature and held that the two were fused to form a third which was neither divine nor human. Christ was thus supposed to be neither God nor man, but possessed of a nature somewhere between the two. But since the divine nature was the greater it followed that for all practical purposes the human was really absorbed into the divine, but with the effect that the divine was also somewhat changed. Eutyches held that two natures implied two persons. Hence he acknowledged in Christ but one life, one intelligence, and one will. Since Eutychianism denied the human element in Christ it denied the real union of God and man and therefore the possibility of an atonement through the human nature. This blending or fusing of the two natures was, of course, the precise opposite of the Nestorian heresy which had so divided the natures as to give a double personality. Eutychianism was too unstable to gain a large following and it was condemned by the Council of Chalcedon in the year 451.

In conclusion, then, we would point out that the orthodox doctrine of the person of Christ has been the common heritage of the Church since the Council of Chalcedon, 451 A. D. It is not a doctrine that was easily arrived at, but one that was worked out only after long and patient study of the Scriptures and after lively debate in the church councils. Numerous other solutions were tried and found wanting. But in this the Church found rest and has continued to rest until our own day. In it alone, it is safe to say, do the Scripture representations of Christ as God and also as man find harmonious

Erroneous Views Concerning the Person of Christ

adjustment. "To the onlooker from this distance of time," says Dr. Warfield, "the main line of the progress of the debate takes on an odd appearance of a steady zigzag advance. Arising out of the embers of the Arian controversy, there is first vigorously asserted, over against the reduction of our Lord to the dimensions of a creature, the pure Deity of His spiritual nature (Apollinarianism); by this there is at once provoked, in the interests of the integrity of our Lord's humanity, the equally vigorous assertion of the completeness of His human nature as the bearer of His Deity (Nestorianism); this in turn provokes, in the interest of the oneness of His person, an equally vigorous assertion of the conjunction of these two natures in a single individuum (Eutychianism): from all of which there gradually emerges at last, by a series of corrections, the balanced statement of Chalcedon, recognizing at once in its 'without confusion, without conversion, eternally and inseparably' the union in the person of Christ of a complete Deity and a complete humanity, constituting a single person without prejudice to the continued integrity of either nature. The pendulum of thought had swung back and forth in ever-decreasing arcs, until at last it found rest along the line of action of the fundamental force. Out of the continuous controversy of a century there issued a balanced statement in which all the elements of the biblical representation were taken up and combined. Work so done is done for all time; and it is capable of ever-repeated demonstation that in the developed doctrine of the Two Natures and in it alone, all the biblical data are brought together in a harmonious statement, in which each receives full recognition, and out of which each may derive its sympathetic exposition. This key unlocks the treasures of the biblical instruction on the person of Christ as none other can, and enables the reader as he currently scans the sacred pages to take up their declarations as they meet him, one after the other, into an intelligently consistent conception of his Lord."[2]

The foregoing survey of the erroneous views concerning the person of Christ would seem to show that history has exhausted the possibilities of heresy and that future denials of the doctrine must be, in essence, only variations of views which have already been advanced and refuted. For, as Dr. A. H. Strong says, "All controversies with regard to the person of Christ must, of necessity, hinge on one of the three points: first, the reality of the two natures; secondly, the integrity of the two natures; thirdly, the union of the two natures in one person. Of these points, Ebionism and Docetism deny the reality of the two natures; Arianism and Apollinarianism deny their integrity; while Nestorianism and Eutychianism deny their proper union. In opposition to all these errors, the orthodox doctrine held its ground and maintains it to this day."[3] And there is much truth in the comment of Dr. A. P. Peabody made in another connection to the effect that "The canon of infidelity was closed almost as soon as that of the Scriptures,"—modern unbelievers having done little more than repeat the long exploded heresies of former centuries. From its earliest origin the Church has believed in both the Deity and the humanity of Christ. Only in the outlawed and comparatively insignificant Ebionite and Docetic sects do we find a belief in a one-natured Christ. Not until the rise of Socianism in the sixteenth century do we find an important defection from the Church doctrine; and that was in substance a recrudescence of the ancient Ebionite heresy which denied the Deity of Christ. Present day Unitarianism and Modernism, which are essentially denials of the supernatural in religion, trace their origin back to that same movement.

---

2. *Christology and Criticism*, p. 264.   3. *Systematic Theology*, p. 672.

XXIII.

CONCLUSION

THUS is portrayed in Scripture the wonderful character of Jesus Christ. It is of the utmost importance that we have right views concerning His person and work. Otherwise we shall never be able to render Him that honor and respect and devotion that He properly deserves, nor shall we be able to understand the system of truth that He has set forth. The question that Christ Himself put to the Pharisees, "What think ye of the Christ? whose Son is He?" is still the critical question, and no one is entitled to the name of Christian who cannot answer that question aright.

What we think of Christ is of supreme importance because our destiny is determined by our attitude toward Him. Within the circle of His redemptive grace is life; all without is death. Those who sincerely accept Him as their Lord and Master are saved and are destined to enjoy an eternity of blessedness. Those who reject Him are lost, and if they persist in that attitude are destined to an eternity of misery and suffering. Scripture and experience unite in affirming that there is no saving knowledge of God apart from Christ, and that all who enter heaven do so only through the atonement that He has provided.

Nothing is more clear than that Christ cannot be explained by any humanistic system. He does not fit into any theory of natural evolution, for in that case the perfect flower of humanity should have appeared at the end of human history and not in the middle of it. Unquestionably His advent was thousands of years too soon to fit that theory. He differs from all other men not only in degree but also in kind. He is, of course, the central figure in the New Testament, and also in the Old when it is read in the light of the New. No explanation other than that He was Deity incarnate is sufficient to account for the majesty of His person and the uplifting influences that have followed wherever His Gospel has been made known.

The advent of Christ has proved to be the central event in all history. Time before His birth is recorded as B. C. (before Christ), and time since as A. D. (*Anno Domino,* in the year of Our Lord). Every time we write a letter, sign a contract, or print a newspaper we state that we are doing so so many years, months and days after the birth of Christ in Bethlehem. And that a mistake of some four years was later discovered to have been made by those who arranged the calendar does not alter the central fact that His advent was the dividing point in history.

A mere glance at the course of history is sufficient to show that at a particular time in the affairs of men a new influence began to be felt and that, despite the slowness with which men have responded, in the midst of all the other kingdoms of the world there has been implanted this ethical and spiritual kingdom which gradually is pervading society and sweetening all its varied forms of life. The contrast between the Christian era and the preceding era has been well expressed by Clarence E. Macartney in the following words: "Do not be misled or deceived by Satanic outbursts of animalism and tyranny and human ferocity, which curse and shadow our world today. In spite of all that, as compared with 'that hard pagan world' into which the Gospel first came, the world today is a world that has been 'turned upside down'. Is the world's labor done today by slaves? Is one-half the population of the world slaves? Are prisoners when taken in battle put to the sword? Are little children exposed and left to die by their parents on the hillsides, and in the forests? Is woman a plaything and chattel of mankind? To ask these questions is to answer them. The power that wrought this great change was the Gospel of Christ. Call up one by one the systems of darkness and tyranny and superstition which have cursed the earth, and which have long since disappeared. Call them out of their graves and ask them, 'Who smote you? What made you pass?' And one by one they answer, 'Christ smote us and we died'."

We sometimes hear Christ mentioned along with Socrates, Plato, Buddha, Confucius, Mohammed, etc., as if He were only one of a class of outstanding leaders or reformers. But even the veriest amateur in spiritual things should know better than to pull Him down to the level of those men. Socrates, perhaps the greatest of the Greeks, was guilty of sinful excesses, even living in open sin with a harlot, and on his death-bed with cold indifference kept his family waiting outside the room while he discussed speculative philosophy with some of his associates. As for Plato, read his *Republic* and discover how low and degrading were his views in regard to the family, slavery, the treatment that men should accord women, etc. Or consider Buddha, withdrawing from mankind instead of sharing their hardships, spending his life in the objective contemplation of the world's ills, and giving rise to a system of morals which are so low that to this day in all Buddhistic countries human values have remained very cheap. Or Confucius, collecting and summarizing the wisdom of the past but essentially atheistic in his outlook and completely lacking of any true appreciation of spiritual values. Or Mohammed, with his well-known polygamous practices, his fiendish cruelty in war, his disdain for all people who were not of his following, and his atrocious system of morals which still lays as a blight on all Moslem lands. No, Christ cannot be put in the same class with the world's supposedly great men. He demands a special category, and cannot be explained on any other grounds than that He was the pure, radiant Son of God. The elements of truth that are found in each of the pagan systems are only borrowed or reflected rays from the Sun of Righteousness. In those systems certain elements of truth are curiously intertwined and confused with fatal error, while in the Christian system these same elements, together with a flood of other truth, are presented in their true relationship and are preserved from all error. When we compare Christian ethics with the best of the codes that have been developed by the Greek, Roman, Chinese, or any other non-Christian philosophers or teachers we see immediately how great is the contrast. In the breadth of their scope, in the motives urged for their practice, and in the fundamental qualities of the precepts themselves the contrast is so striking that no serious critics even pretend that there is any real comparison.

Through all the weary centuries man apart from God has never been able to find peace. But in Christ he does find peace and is acutely aware that he has passed out of death into life. The tragic fact, however, is that under the influence of Modernism, materialistic evolution, and so-called higher criticism many of our present day churches have lost much of their witnessing power. The words of Dr. A. H. Strong, written a generation ago, seem even more applicable today. "Many of our teachers and preachers," said he, "have swung off into a practical denial of Christ's deity and of His atonement. We seem upon the verge of a second Unitarian defection that will break up churches and compel secessions, in a worse manner than did that of Channing and Ware a century ago. American Christianity recovered from that disaster only by vigorously asserting the authority of Christ and the inspiration of the Scriptures. We need a new vision of the Saviour like Paul saw on the way to Damascus and John saw on the isle of Patmos, to convince us that Jesus is lifted above space and time, and that His existence antedated creation, that He conducted the march of Hebrew history, that He was born of a virgin, suffered on the cross, rose from the dead, and now lives forevermore, the Lord of the universe, the only God with whom we have to do, our Saviour here and our Judge hereafter. Without a revival of this faith our churches will become secularized, mission enterprise will die out, and the candlestick will be removed out of its place as it was with the seven churches of Asia, and as it has been with the apostate churches of New England."

What a marvelous person is this Christ of the Ages! Every true Christian should be a witness for his Lord and Master, and his witness in order to be effective should be corroborated by a consistently upright manner of life. It is both our duty and privilege to tell others of this wonderful Saviour and of the redemption that has been purchased for them by Him. For His Gospel is the answer to all of the world's ills; and above and beyond that it is the power of God unto salvation to every one that believeth, our ground of comfort and our hope of glory. Would that this vision might be clearly presented to every human being on the whole face of the earth, and that mankind in general might come to realize the poverty that is theirs without Christ and the joy that might be their's with Christ.

THE END

www.ingramcontent.com/pod-product-compliance
Lightning Source LLC
Chambersburg PA
CBHW050147170426
43197CB00011B/1993